English coursework

Philip Gooden teaches in the
School, Bath, and is the auth
Notes.

Also available:

English coursework: **Drama and Poetry**
English coursework: **Prose**

Brodie's Notes on
English coursework
Conflict

Philip Gooden BA

Pan Books London, Sydney and Auckland

First published 1991 by Pan Books Ltd,
Cavaye Place, London SW10 9PG

9 8 7 6 5 4 3 2 1

© Pan Books Ltd 1991

ISBN 0 330 50310 3

Photoset by Parker Typesetting Service, Leicester

Printed and bound in Great Britain by
Clays Ltd, St Ives plc, Bungay, Suffolk

This book is sold subject to the condition that it shall not,
by way of trade or otherwise, be lent, re-sold, hired out
or otherwise circulated without the publisher's prior consent
in any form of binding or cover other than that in which
it is published and without a similar condition including this
condition being imposed on the subsequent purchaser

Conflict

Texts used in this book

Achebe *Things Fall Apart* 46–47
Barstow *A Kind of Loving* 38–39
Bolt *A Man for All Seasons* 29–30
Charlotte Brontë *Jane Eyre* 30–32
Chatwin *On the Black Hill* 44–46
Cormier *The Chocolate War* 19–20
Dickens *Great Expectations* 20–24
 A Tale of Two Cities 49–52
Golding *Lord of the Flies* 17–19
Hall *The Long and the Short and the Tall* 58–59
Heaney 'Digging' 34–35
Hersey *Hiroshima* 66
D. H. Lawrence *The Daughter-in-Law* 36–37
 Sons and Lovers 35–37
Harper Lee *To Kill a Mockingbird* 41–42
Miller *The Crucible* 29–30
Orwell *Nineteen Eighty-Four* 52–54
Owen 'Dulce et Decorum Est' 61–62
 'Exposure' 60
 'The Next War' 62
 'The Send-Off' 60–61
Pope *The Rape of the Lock* 4–5
Priestley *An Inspector Calls* 37–38
Sassoon 'Base Details' 60
 'The General' 59–60
 Memoirs of an Infantry Officer 62–63
Shakespeare *Henry V* 55–56
 Julius Caesar 24–26
 Macbeth 11–15, 33–34
 The Merchant of Venice 6–8, 42–44
Sheriff *Journey's End* 57–59
Stevenson *Dr Jekyll and Mr Hyde* 15–16
Swift *Gulliver's Travels* 68–69
Thomas 'As the Team's Head Brass' 63–64
Twain *Huckleberry Finn* 27–28
Wyndham *The Chrysalids* 67

(Note: very brief references are not included.)
See page 75 for the list of relevant Brodie's Notes on the above texts. These will help you with detail on your coursework and increase your knowledge of the book concerned.

Contents

Preface by the general editor ix

Introduction
Conflict in the news 1
The key features of conflict 3
Conflict in literature 4
Ways of approaching the subject 8

Internal conflict
Good and evil 11
Divided loyalties 20
Questions of life and death 28
Love versus duty 30

External conflict
General introduction 33
Group conflict: family and class 34
Group conflict: race and culture 41
Revolution and rebellion 48
War: a chivalrous conflict 54
War: the modern view 57
War: nuclear conflict 66

Summing up 68

General questions 71

Some suggested further reading 73

Relevant Brodie's Notes 75

Preface by the general editor

The thematic approach to the study of literature has long been practised by teachers, and this new series of Brodie's Notes focuses on areas of investigation which will help teachers and students at GCSE and A-level alike.

The Notes will stimulate disciplined and imaginative involvement with your chosen books by widening your horizons to the possibility of studying works which are comparable in theme (say, Conflict) or genre (say, the Short Story).

Do not get so absorbed that you see *only* the theme under discussion and nothing else: the theme of any book – whether the presentation of marriage, or of love, or of conflict – is only a part of the whole. Read primarily to enjoy and discover, and try to work out how important the theme you are examining is to the whole: it may reside in character or situation or social conditions or any number of areas. One thing is sure: by recognizing and appreciating the theme or themes you will have learned more about the work you are studying. As a result you will be able to write about it more fully, and place it in a broader literary context.

The editor of each Theme/Genre Note in this series is an experienced teacher, and his or her aim is to promote your interest in a range of ideas and books – whether prose, drama or poetry, at the same time extending your capacity for literary appreciation and your imaginative participation in what you read.

For more specific help, you can refer to Brodie's Notes on individual texts.

Graham Handley 1991

Introduction

Conflict in the news

Look at the headlines in today's newspaper, watch this evening's news on television. It is a near certainty that the principal story on the front page or on the screen will be to do with conflict between human beings. It may be a war, or the threat of one; civil disturbance; protests; a battle of words in a court of law; an argument among members of opposed political parties, or a slanging match among factions involved in an industrial dispute.

Turn to the back pages of the newspaper, wait until the end of the news broadcast, and you see reports on what is the most popular and acceptable form of human conflict: sport. A football match is a kind of ritualized battle, often reflected by the almost equally ritualized hostility between supporters of opposing teams. Most sports abound in military-style talk of 'manoeuvres', 'campaigns', 'tactics' and 'strategy'. Matches and fixtures are referred to as competitions, but the line between 'competition' and 'conflict' is indeterminate and therefore easy to cross. Anybody who has seen a fight break out on the field between rival members of the sides concerned knows how quickly what was merely a 'game' turns violently serious.

Even the gossipy, scandalous material which makes up the bulk of some newspapers is frequently touched by conflict. Domestic dramas, divorces, agonized separations, a 'tug of love' between parents over a child, all have at their root a clash of individuals or groups. Almost everything that comes to us under the heading of 'news', whether important or trivial, has to do with this fundamental aspect of human nature and society.

We might treat lightly the examples of conflict given above. After all, the news media are in the business of ransacking the world for exciting stories: inevitably they will focus on wars, disputes, turbulence, because a good fight or a proper argument make for exciting television and dramatic headlines. Even if events are not exaggerated or distorted by the presence of the media itself, the prevailing impression we receive is of a world torn by hostility and competitiveness. Daily reality is surely different and duller.

English coursework: Conflict

But any consideration of ourselves, our own lives, shows that conflict is inescapable here too. Every time an individual argues seriously with himself over whether he should or shouldn't do something, he is experiencing an inner conflict. Rows in a family, between the different generations, or among children, are examples of external conflict. A playground fight, a quarrel over how late a teenager can stay out at night, a dispute with neighbours who play their music too loud, a difference of opinion about your change in a shop, a shouting match over which television channel to watch; all are instances of local conflict, the kind of thing each of us is familiar with in everyday life.

Life might be pleasanter without some, or all, of these small conflicts. But such a life is also almost unimaginable. A world in which there are no wars, no racial hatreds, no religious persecutions, no battles between parents and children, no fights – spiritual, verbal, physical, psychological – of *any* kind, is a world in which there are no people. It is significant that in order to envisage a world free of conflict we have to go either very far forward or very far back: forward to some science-fiction vision of the future in which mankind has 'outgrown' its warring instincts, or back to a mythical past in which humanity lived in perfect harmony with itself and with the world, as in the Garden of Eden. Such visions are dreams or fables. They are consoling or imaginatively stimulating, but they don't have much to do with reality. By this response we show our awareness that conflict, in some form or other, is an unavoidable part of being human. Because we are all individuals who choose to (or have to) live in groups, each of us – however patient or selfless – is bound to find his or her wishes sometimes in conflict with those of others in the group. This is true at the level of the family, the school, the neighbourhood, the area, right up to the level of the nation and the power bloc. From before the moment of birth we are equipped with the resources to make our wants known. The baby cries because it wants to be fed, to be attended to: if it didn't behave like this there would be something wrong. But our needs, from the time that we are born, will frequently be in conflict with the needs of those around us.

The key features of conflict

Conflict is basic, and necessary, to human existence. We wouldn't be where we are without it. We probably wouldn't be here at all – nor would any other form of life, except the most rudimentary. However much the nineteenth-century theories of the evolution of life on earth have been modified, there is general acceptance that the notion of conflict or struggle (between members of different species, between a species and its environment) is a valid one in helping us to understand how complex life developed.

Conflict, of course, can be enjoyable. Most people enjoy taking part in contests of some kind, even if only card or board games, where there is an element of ritualized conflict or hostility; 'ritualized' because each side, though wanting to beat the other, agrees to be governed by predetermined rules of 'fair play'. Most of us enjoy too watching others involved in conflicts of some sort, even those in which we ourselves would prefer not to participate. Court-room dramas naturally fascinate an audience, whether the people in the public gallery at the Old Bailey watching a real case or in a cinema or theatre watching a fictional one. The more that hangs on the outcome of a case the more gripping it will be for the spectators. Yet few people would want to change places with the accused in the dock. We take pleasure in watching or reading about fictional fights (verbal, physical, etc) that we would do our utmost to escape from in real life. And of course we relish conflict in real life too – not the kind involving outright war or widespread destruction (although there is fascination even in this) but the kind that can be accurately summed up by 'a good fight'. The expression is usually applied to a contest or struggle that brings us satisfaction at the skill or strength of the participants. The pleasure will be greater if we feel that the 'right' participant has won, the one showing the greater expertise, the one whom we consider to have right on his side, or, more simply, the one with whom we happen to identify. But it is the battle itself that also engages us, not just the question of whether the right side will be victorious. Our pleasure springs from a natural competitiveness or aggression in human nature. Seeing these traits exhibited by others (in real life or in fiction) is both stimulating and, perhaps, satisfying for the onlooker.

Not everything, of course, is shaped or distorted by conflict. It would be a mistake to apply the term indiscriminately. Small differences of opinion with a friend, or an argument with oneself over something trivial (that extra helping of food, maybe), don't deserve to be dignified with the title of 'conflict'. Indeed the term is already wide enough, encompassing as it does anything from a contest between individuals to a world war. The word 'conflict' comes with a certain seriousness attached. To be in a state of conflict, with oneself or with others, is to be at odds with an opposing force in a way that suggests that each side recognizes a significance to the struggle. The penalty for failure will probably be acutely felt; risk to life, even its loss, may be involved. Damage to something less tangible, such as pride or reputation, will almost certainly be part of the price paid by the loser.

It is apparent from this that what matters in a conflict, and one of the signs to look for so as to ensure that we are using the term correctly, is not the outward importance of the event that has prompted the conflict but the inner, subjective feelings and assessments brought to it by the various participants. A couple of the examples cited earlier are apparently minor: the quarrel with neighbours who throw their windows open and turn their music up in the summer; the disagreement over whether you have received the correct change in a shop. But the feelings brought to these encounters are often out of all proportion to their causes.

Conflict in literature

The point is well illustrated in *The Rape of the Lock* by the eighteenth-century poet, Alexander Pope. This poem was prompted by a quarrel that had arisen between two aristocratic families over the behaviour of a member of one towards a member of the other: he had cut off a lock of her hair when she was distracted by the 'fragrant steams' emanating from a cup of coffee. The act of 'rape', here in the sense of a forcible taking, is unimportant – to a detached observer the fuss that follows is ridiculous. Around this slight incident Pope fashions several hundred lines of poetry, a very elaborate artificial piece of work. The poem is built on the disproportion between the event itself, the 'rape', and the uproar which it stirred up. By treating the 'crime' with immense but ironic gravity Pope is attempting to laugh it out of existence. The very fact that he chose to bring to bear such a complicated apparatus on something so simple as the snipping off of a few strands of hair indicates that the breach between the two families was a serious one, absurd though its origins were. A moment's reflection tells us that the bitterest quarrels are often over the smallest things. As Pope puts it at the beginning of *The Rape of the Lock*:

What dire Offence from am'rous Causes springs,
What mighty Contests rise from trivial things.

Conflict, then, is to be comprehended not so much in terms of the external factors that provoke it but instead by the strength and complexity of the emotions generated.

The key word here is 'emotions'. At the human level conflict must entail feeling. One can use the term 'intellectual conflict' or 'moral conflict' and conceive such struggles as being between two impersonal forces. But the moment one visualizes the struggle as being between individuals (or groups of them) emotion enters. An example: two scientists offering differing theories about the same phenomenon may be said to be in 'intellectual conflict'. If one, or both, could honestly claim that he didn't mind whether his theory was proved right or not, his only concern being that the truth is discovered, then the term 'conflict' hardly applies. The scientist has submerged his own personal needs (for self-esteem, for public acclaim, etc) in the general search for the truth. There is no 'conflict' here, rather there is co-operation. If, however, the scientist has some emotional investment in what is *his* idea – and he would hardly be human if he didn't – then he can be said to be in 'conflict' with his partner or rival because he has something to lose (pride, applause, etc) if he is proved wrong. To sum up: a conflict is a clash – of opinions, wills, interests, feelings, and so on – in which each side has invested significance and in which each perceives there to be some penalty for failure.

Conflict is therefore central to literature and to drama. It is hard to conceive of a stage play that would not necessitate conflict on some level, rather as it is hard to imagine a world in which there might be no disagreements or hostility. Fiction, in particular the novel, with its especial capacity for examining at length the motivating forces within the individual, demands friction or the sense of opposition for a narrative to be sustained.

English coursework: Conflict

There has to be something for the central character(s) to operate on, something to react against, something or somebody that gets in the way.

The benefits of reading about or watching situations involving conflict go far beyond the simple thrill of seeing other (imaginary) people caught up in predicaments which we might rather not undergo ourselves. Witnessing fictional events on stage or screen, reading about them, gives us the opportunity to experience some of the emotions, responses, uncertainties and confusions displayed by the characters involved. Our reactions will not be as strong as the original emotions, of course, but they will be related to them in ways that are both complex and, often, hard to analyse. An effective book, play or film should raise emotions of some kind in the attentive reader or audience. It may leave us informed, but if it also leaves us quite untouched, then it might as well be a car maintenance manual – and either it has failed in its job or we have been insufficiently responsive.

Our response may be quite complicated and unsettled. Shakespeare's *Merchant of Venice* provides a good introduction here. The play's most interesting character is Shylock, a Jewish money-lender. Shylock strikes a bargain, which at first sounds as though it is meant to be a joke rather than a proper contract, whereby a Christian Venetian who borrows money from him will forfeit a pound of flesh (literally) if he does not repay the money within a specified period. Naturally things go wrong, and Shylock is inclined to exact his pound of flesh. At this point Shakespeare gives him a speech in which he asserts the humanity which Jews share with all other human beings; in part it reads:

Hath not a Jew eyes? hath not a Jew hands, organs, dimensions, senses, affections, passions? fed with the same food, hurt with the same weapons, subject to the same diseases, healed by the same means, warmed and cooled by the same winter and summer, as a Christian is? – if you prick us, do we not bleed? if you tickle us do we not laugh? if you poison us, do we not die? (III,1).

The words are persuasive. They are delivered by a man who, by accident of birth and race, finds himself in conflict with the Christian society in which he makes a despised living. Taking these lines in isolation, as they are often taken, makes us feel the reasonableness of Shylock's plea.

But when the speech is heard in full our response may be more complex. Shylock continues, after the passage quoted above:

> ... and if you wrong us shall we not revenge? – if we are like you in the rest, we will resemble you in that. If a Jew wrong a Christian, what is his humility? revenge! If a Christian wrong a Jew, what should his sufferance be by Christian example? – why revenge.

The money-lender's argument is that the Venetian Christians, and specifically Antonio (the Merchant of the title), treat him with contempt and, far from following Christ's example of humility, of 'turning the other cheek', practise a policy of revenge. If Shylock is a man like them in all other particulars, why should he be different in this? In other words, he is asserting his right to be a human being and to show it by behaving inhumanely. He is not so much making a plea for racial tolerance (which is how the speech is sometimes interpreted), as saying, in effect: 'You taught me how to behave badly and now you'll find out how well I have learned that lesson!'

Our reaction to Shylock's speech is likely, if we have been properly receptive, to be one of uncertainty, even confusion. Shakespeare invites us to share Shylock's sense of resentment at being an outcast, but we are surely not intended to condone his desire for revenge even though we may understand it. On one level, then, we may condemn this character – and the likelihood is that Shakespeare's audience would have, in strong terms – while on another level we are urged to feel *with* him. We are given a brief, heartfelt glimpse of what it is like to be human yet denied full membership of the human society in which one finds oneself (the essence of racial or religious intolerance), yet at the same time Shylock reminds us that he is only too similar to the Christian members of that society in seeking revenge; in a sense he is no outcast at all.

Shylock is a character in conflict, by birth and by choice, with the community where he has a marginal, unwelcome place. But the feelings which the money-lender rouses in *us* are also conflicting ones. It may be that by the end of the play we are unable to arrive at a final and absolute judgement on this intriguing figure. Conflict is therefore not something restricted to the stage (or the page or the screen). It spills over into the response of reader or audience, at least in a work of any complexity. With a fictional character in conflict with himself, with others, with his surroundings, we may feel not only something of his experience at second hand (Shylock's indignation at the way he is treated by Christians), but also realize a divided response within ourselves: is Shylock justified? should he display mercy towards a man who has never shown him tolerance?

It must be stressed that such a conflict of views is inevitable and desirable. Our own ideas develop only if they are tested against those of other people. In discussion and argument, including argument with ourselves, we modify, sometimes change altogether, our opinions. Ideas which we hold because they have been handed over to us by those people we like or respect may be perfectly good ideas, but they are unlikely to be properly ours until they have been tested in 'conflict' with opposing theories.

Ways of approaching the subject

Conflict is recognized as a vital component of human evolution and indeed of all life. Permeating the whole range of human activity – from schoolwork to space-shots – are concepts such as 'competition', 'striving', 'ambition', 'challenge', which take for granted an underlying conflict between individuals, or nations, or humanity and its environment. We acknowledge war as the most futile and wasteful form of conflict (this is particularly evident in the work of the poets of World War I, some of which will be discussed later in this book), yet even here it is not impossible to see benefits springing from unlikely sources. Advances in medicine, scientific discovery, some social progress, all can be discerned in the desperate circumstances of the world-wide conflicts earlier in this century. And art of all kinds thrives on conflict – of theories, of practices – as well as drawing enormous quantities of material from conflict itself.

When you are discussing and writing about plays, stories, films, you will therefore find yourself dealing inevitably with conflict. Try to decide what type of conflict you are dealing with. Is it internal or external, or both? Does an author give us an insight into a character to show us that he or she is battling with him or herself, or is the author concerned only with *external* opposition between his various creations? How easy or difficult is it to decide who has 'right' on their side in a contest? Are we meant to experience a mixed response (as in the case of Shylock in *The Merchant of Venice*), or have we just failed to sort out our own feelings? Go back to the text and look for evidence to support your point of view. See whether you can find opposing views of an individual, a situation, a dilemma. Ought you to attach equal weight to everything everybody says in a novel or play? It should be apparent that when one is trying to describe and assess a situation involving conflict, in a novel or a drama, one is as a judge, taking in as much of the 'evidence' as possible, attempting to be fair, responding properly to the complexity of things. But our feelings, as audience or readers, are also involved. They have to be worked into the picture. A personal response to a piece of literature is worth a quantity of dry, passionless description – as long as that response is the result of genuine consideration.

Other questions arise in relation to our reactions. What makes for the more interesting reading or viewing – a situation in which there is a clearly defined 'right' side and 'wrong' side, or one in which motives and justifications are shared between different parties to a dispute? Why is it possible, even easy, to sympathize with or be attracted by a 'bad' character or argument (look at the popularity of certain figures in horror films) and what conflict does such a sympathy raise within us? Examine your responses and be prepared to argue with yourself, without feeling that you have to reach a cut-and-dried answer.

This study looks at the theme of conflict from the centre outwards, as it were, beginning with conflict in the starkest and most obvious form – the choice between good and evil – and locating that choice within the individual. From there we move to the more familiar choices that everybody faces: choices between, say, opposing loyalties or conflicting desires – alternatives which may not have the same dramatic clarity as that between 'right' and 'wrong' but which nevertheless involve conflict and uncertainty. This is followed by some discussion of external conflict, ranging from that within families to hostility between classes or races, to the ultimate form of conflict and that which has naturally stimulated much writing (and art of all kinds): war.

It should be emphasized at the start that the theme has been cut up into segments like this for convenience and ease of reading. In reality, and in fiction, conflict does not remain

English coursework: Conflict

happily in one compartment. Internal conflict is almost bound to manifest itself in some external fashion, as the opening discussion of *Macbeth* illustrates. One type of hostility can easily slide into another; racial and religious persecution may go hand in hand; either can be the basis of wars between nations. Don't assume that you have discovered all you can when you've decided what 'type' of conflict is under study. Equally, don't assume that everything you read or see can be stamped 'conflict'. It is a vital component, sometimes healthy, sometimes destructive, of human nature and human society – but it's not the only one!

Internal conflict

Good and evil

The clash between good and evil has an inevitable dramatic force. While the fact of evil troubles thinkers and theologians its existence is a godsend for the writer or dramatist. Good and evil stand in stark contrast, as plainly opposed as wrestlers or boxers in their respective corners of the ring. There is the same prospect of a good fight, and a simple satisfaction in identifying the 'good' and the 'bad' and watching each side perform in accordance with its own nature.

Colourful evil, or villainy, will have its own appeal. A Dracula or a Frankenstein, the arch-criminal in a James Bond story, all have a dynamic quality that catches our interest and may even enlist our sympathy. It is the same impulse that encourages children to hiss at the villain in a pantomime: not from hatred or fear but from appreciation of someone who is rather good at his (bad) business. Such conflicts between villain and hero are appreciated on a very simple level: and we know it is safe to hiss the villain because we realize that he is certain to lose. It is one of the conventions of the genre (pantomime, spy thriller, detective story) that evil will eventually be defeated. Reality is different. If we examine a work that demands considerably more than this response we see that the problem of evil – including its glamour – is dealt with in a fashion that permits us to feel that we are offered something both exciting and emotionally and psychologically valid.

Macbeth (1606)

Of all Shakespeare's tragedies *Macbeth* is the only one in which the protagonist makes a deliberate choice between good and evil and suffers as a consequence the conflict, inner and outer, throughout the play. The main action of the drama unfolds from the point at which the idea of murder first thrills Macbeth. But from its beginning the play is concerned with conflict. A battle is taking place off-stage during the opening scenes, and our introduction to Macbeth is as a warrior, a ruthlessly efficient fighter. Shakespeare's preoccupation, however, is not so much with the tragic hero's military prowess as with the contradictions in his character.

Macbeth, returning from the battlefield with his ally Banquo, meets the witches who prophesy that he will become King of Scotland. His reaction is of key significance. It is signalled to the audience *before Macbeth has said anything*. His posture, even his facial expression, must fit Banquo's words:

Good Sir, why do you start, and seem to fear
Things that do sound so fair? (I,3)

Later on Banquo describes him as being 'rapt'. Macbeth has shrunk into himself. His first proper comments on the witches' predictions are an aside, that is, they are not intended to be shared with any other character on stage. The great isolation that will overtake Macbeth has already begun. He is engaged in a horrified debate with himself. What do the prophecies mean? Are they good or bad? He cannot decide: 'This supernatural soliciting/Cannot be ill; cannot be good'. Macbeth is not even sure of the quality of his physical responses, let alone the worth of what the witches have said. If the predictions are good, he asks himself,

... why do I yield to that suggestion
Whose horrid image doth unfix my hair,
And make my seated heart knock at my ribs,
Against the use of nature?

His heart beats unnaturally fast in fearful excitement. Or is it excited fear? Both responses are present in the prospect: the murder of a king. One part of him recoils from murder, another is seduced by it. Nor are the twin preoccupations, of murder and of becoming king, separable. To become king is to turn murderer. It is interesting that Macbeth does not at this stage consider other routes to the throne; only later when his excitement has subsided does he seem content to leave things to 'chance'.

Here then is an emotional conflict in which instinctive responses – of horror, of attraction – are at war with each other. It would be difficult to get to a more elemental level of conflict. Shakespeare, having dealt briefly with a bloody battle between armies at the beginning of the play, is now focusing on the

Internal conflict

soundless, bloodless, but equally important battle *within* the individual. The clash in this scene is between the good and evil in Macbeth, if we identify his abhorrence of the murder with the former and his being drawn towards it with the latter.

The first Act provides another instance of inner conflict when Macbeth once more debates with himself the killing of Duncan, who by a stroke of fortune (good or bad?) is spending the night with his entourage at Macbeth's castle. In a soliloquy (I,7) Macbeth itemizes the arguments against murder: that the king is his guest and under his protection, that the king is a good man, and so on. Against these Macbeth can set only his violent ambition. Here is a 'cold' conflict, as it were – 'cold' because Macbeth's reasoning is laid out in a fairly temperate and methodical manner – which can be contrasted with the horrified confusion which he discovers within himself after the encounter with the witches. Yet even here Macbeth's tangled thoughts are captured by the coiling phrasing of the opening of his speech: here he meditates on the chances of getting away with it, unpunished in this world.

If it were done, when 'tis done, then 'twere well
It were done quickly: if th'assassination
Could trammel up the consequence, and catch
With his surcease success . . .

He is pessimistic about this, and his fear of the consequences of the murder together with his respect for Duncan enable him to reach a resolution by the time Lady Macbeth enters: 'We will proceed no further in this business'. However, no sooner has he argued himself out of murder than he is urged into it again by his wife. At this point the fight becomes externalized, and a quarrel breaks out between the couple. Lady Macbeth taunts her warrior husband with cowardice; their dispute turns on conflicting definitions of 'manhood'. Macbeth considers that there are some actions which do not 'become' or suit a man (i.e. are unmanly) while Lady Macbeth claims that, given that he has already conspired with her to carry out the murder, to fail to turn words into deeds is to demonstrate weakness. We know that she has won when he asks the simple but all-important question, 'If we should fail?' . . . The argument has shifted from a moral level to a practical one. Not, 'Is this a right action?' but: 'Is this something we can expect to get away with?'

English coursework: Conflict

The conflict that Macbeth embodies – and this is, of course, only one aspect of the play as a whole – spreads both inward and outward. Opposition to his reign grows as he grows more tyrannical, and the final quarter of the action is given over to the advance of the forces of the 'rebels' (in fact, the supporters of the legitimate heir to the throne, King Duncan's son) and to Macbeth's increasingly desperate but self-defeating efforts to preserve himself. The conflict within Macbeth, now King of Scotland, undergoes an interesting alteration. No longer does he debate explicitly the morality of murder. After a couple of killings he is committed to the bloody path, a prospect that fills him not with the grim excitement he felt at first but with tedium. All he can relish now is his own ruthlessness. Yet traces of the conflict between right and wrong are still there. Macbeth suffers for his wrong choice, and for the wrong choices he continues to make (although all his subsequent acts flow from the murder of Duncan). Every vicious act designed to secure his position succeeds, ironically, only in undermining it. He is shaken by nightmares, he cannot eat in peace (the ghost of his one-time ally Banquo returns to shatter the feast designed to celebrate his accession to the throne): sound sleep and untroubled eating represent the vital elements of the ordinary life which Macbeth is unable to live.

Worst of all, Macbeth has reduced his existence to a matter of insignificance, a thing devoid of moral weight. Incapable of taking anything seriously except his desire to go on living, however unhappily (here we sense that he envies the peace of those he has put to death), Macbeth destroys himself morally. Making Scotland into a kind of desert, a place hostile to decent life, he lays waste his own existence, and it is one of Shakespeare's most profound achievements to convince us that the greatest act of destruction which Macbeth accomplishes within the play is his own. The conflict that brings the tragic hero to this final point is an inner one, in which his own outraged conscience manifests itself in horrific visions and a frenzied search for a position of security, something that eludes him the more he reaches.

Assignments

1 '*Macbeth* contains evidence of supernatural evil in its witches, and its horrific visions, but the real evil lies within the human characters.' Do you agree?

Suggested notes for your answer: Witches don't make Macbeth evil – they bring to surface murderous traits within his personality (why does he think *first* of killing, not of some legitimate way of becoming king?) – Macbeth has *choice*, at one point he nearly abandons his plans – Lady Macbeth deliberately chooses evil over good (find supporting quotations from her first speeches in the play) – both husband and wife are thrilled by notion of evil, by discovery of unsuspected capacity within themselves for brutality – outward manifestations of evil are flashy, designed to make our flesh creep (look at list of ingredients that witches put into their cauldron) – Shakespeare's concern is with inner evil, its glamour and danger.

2 In a brief interlude of sanity before her death Lady Macbeth writes to her husband, reviewing their life together. What does she say?

3 How would you stage the scenes involving the witches – lighting, costumes, 'atmosphere'? (Don't go for the obvious!)

4 Find another text that involves a choice made by a character between good and evil, and compare it with *Macbeth*.

Jekyll and Hyde (1886)

Macbeth allows his evil side to dominate, and Shakespeare shows the self-destructive properties of that evil. The idea that in human beings there is the capacity to do bad as well as good, and that these aspects will often be at war with each other, is a very old and familiar one. This concept was carried to an extreme by Robert Louis Stevenson in his short novel *The Strange Case of Dr Jekyll and Mr Hyde*. The principal character here is really two. The scientist Henry Jekyll, already conscious from an early age of 'man's dual nature', manufactures and swallows a drug which, in effect, severs his good side from his bad, creating two where there was one. As Edward Hyde he is violent and vindictive, enjoying cruelty in a casual way (he tramples on a child in the street, he clubs an old man to death). After each night's excursion, when the drug wears off, he is transformed into the respectable and professional figure of Dr Jekyll. The power and the interest of this famous fantasy spring from the fact that it answers an awareness that most people have that there are competing strains inside them – creative and destructive, kind and hurtful. Stevenson seizes on this and pushes it to the limit by artificially separating contending passions that were housed in a single body. The novel also plays on our fears of loss of self-control, fears that a side of our personality which we prefer to keep suppressed might force its way to the surface. This is what occurs at the end of *Dr Jekyll and Mr Hyde*. Jekyll discovers that he can no longer control his transformations – a delight becomes a waking nightmare. He is half dozing when:

> in one of my more wakeful moments, my eye fell upon my hand. Now, the hand of Henry Jekyll ... was professional in shape and size; it was large, firm, white and comely. But the hand which I now saw, clearly enough in the yellow light of a mid-London morning, lying half shut on the bed-clothes, was lean, corded, knuckly, of a dusky pallor, and thickly shaded with a swart growth of hair. It was the hand of Edward Hyde.

The evil here is given a concrete, external manifestation. The scene, like several in *Dr Jekyll and Mr Hyde*, has the sensational quality of a horror movie (it isn't surprising that the novel has been filmed several times). In a way, this is a consoling depiction of evil because it suggests that it is something 'out there', abnormal, beyond the run of ordinary experience. Henry Jekyll conforms to a popular stereotype (the 'mad scientist'), and only an obsessed individual, touched by madness, would choose to behave as he does. Macbeth, by contrast, is in many respects an ordinary man: he is sensitive about taunts of cowardice, he is quite capable of coming to a decision and then being pushed in a different direction moments later, he deludes himself into believing that everything will be all right if only he takes one final step to safeguard his position. Macbeth does not alter his appearance and turn grotesque, even at his most corrupt. He is a man, not a monster, and that is ultimately what makes *Macbeth* more frightening and more penetrating as a study of evil than Stevenson's (admittedly much less ambitious) work.

Lord of the Flies (1954) and *The Chocolate War* (1975)

Arguably more troubling presentations of the conflict between good and evil appear in two modern novels, both about children and adolescents, by William Golding and Robert Cormier. Both are pessimistic books, in part because they take a period of life – schooldays – usually associated with innocence, or at least with harmlessness, and demonstrate persuasively that evil and corruption are as rife in the hearts of the young as they are in adults. In fact the absence of adult authority is a disturbing factor in each story.

Golding's *Lord of the Flies*, one of the most famous and influential novels of the last fifty years, has acquired a mythlike status in its dramatization of what happens to a group of schoolboys who find themselves alone on a desert island. At first their spirits are high – it is wonderful to be left in a world unbothered by the grown-ups! Ralph, one of the natural leaders of the group, lays down the rules by which their primitive but not undemocratic 'society' should be governed. But the effort to maintain standards is painful. Slowly the skin of civilization is peeled away as the boys are seduced by the more attractive way of life held out by Jack, Ralph's rival. Jack offers the simple satisfaction of belonging to a gang and of organized hunting. The gang, which requires enemies (or non-members) to give it a sense of identity, gradually replaces the community that began to evolve in the early stages of the story. The hunting is pursued partly for the practical purpose of getting meat – there are wild pigs on the island. But it quickly becomes clear that hunting meets a deeper and darker need. The excitement of the pursuit and the kill turns into sadistic relish, and it is not surprising that in the climax Ralph, completely deserted, finds himself the human quarry of a murderous chase.

The novel is complex and poetic; it should not be read as a simple enactment of the battle between good and evil. For one thing, the line between the two is hard to draw. When does boyish exuberance become malevolence? At what point does a seemingly innocent activity, like daubing faces with clay for camouflage, slide into something sinister? Jack, the boy who is the first to realize the potential of a 'painted' face to conceal himself from the pigs he hunts, is delighted by the 'mask' provided by the coloured clays. He is liberated by it. But the boyish play with this face-paint – only an extension of a child's dressing up – has a nasty underside. Jack 'began to dance and his laughter became a bloodthirsty snarling'. It is a world in which it is hard to locate the moment at which 'laughter' becomes 'snarling', at which the civilized surrenders to the primitive – it is significant that at a late stage Ralph says to the small remnant of his followers: '"Well, we won't be painted ... because we aren't savages."' He shows a clear intuition that seemingly childish painting covers wickedness.

In the first two texts discussed, *Macbeth* and *Dr Jekyll and Mr Hyde*, evil was presented as something attractive but clear-cut. Without being able to foresee all the consequences the protagonists nevertheless knew what they were doing when they embarked on a corrupt course. Golding's picture in *Lord of the Flies* is shadowy by comparison. It is not that evil is not indisputably present on the island, it is rather that the boys suppose it outside themselves and create fearful, imaginary 'beasts' that must be fought against or placated like pagan gods. The boys are, of course, incapable of the kind of self-analysis which Macbeth applies. But they are 'innocent' only in the sense that they don't truly know themselves. There is no moment of choice when the majority 'decides' to turn savage. It is instead a creeping process in which good and evil are entwined in a complex way.

As an indication of this complexity, take the image of fire. It is a near obsession with Ralph that the boys must keep a fire going so that the smoke will signal their presence on the island to any passing ship. But the discipline and co-operative effort required to maintain the fire break down. There are more exciting priorities, like hunting and having 'fun'. In this aspect therefore the fire – or rather its maintenance – might stand for the (doomed) attempt to hold to a civilized order. And we might remember that the discovery of fire marked one of the very earliest stages in man's development. At two points in the narrative, however, there are episodes describing fires out of control; the first (in Chapter Two, 'Fire on the Mountain') started accidentally, the second (in the final chapter) started deliberately. The hunters mean to 'smoke out' Ralph, and in doing so they 'set the island on fire'. The destructive rapidity of the blaze echoes the spread of bloodthirstiness and fear among the children as all 'adult' standards of civilized behaviour are at last thrown away.

Internal conflict

The fire is here a mirror of the rage to destroy which burns inside the gang. Yet fire, domesticated and controlled, is necessary to any attempt at civilized life; the boys need it to cook food, they use fire as a focal point for their community life. The concept of fire in *Lord of the Flies* is a mobile one; it suggests different values at different times in the narrative or, less simply, it can point to different, even conflicting things at the same moment.

This brief description of the fire concept in Golding's novel illustrates the difficulty of disentangling the positive from the negative, the 'good' elements from 'bad' ones. The co-existence of both in the children on the island, and the eventual dominance of inner corruption, are made grimly manifest. At the exhausted and sombre close of the story Ralph weeps for his awareness of 'the end of innocence, the darkness of man's heart'. He has grown up, but maturity brings no pleasure. It is worth noting in this context that the novel first appeared in 1954: that is, at an early point in the nuclear age (it is significant that the boys have crash-landed on the island while being evacuated from England because of some man-made catastrophe, probably a nuclear exchange). In addition, *Lord of the Flies* came out less than a decade after the conclusion of the Second World War and the discovery of the Nazi concentration camps, the most pessimistic witness to 'the darkness of man's heart'.

Robert Cormier's *The Chocolate War* deals too with the enclosed lives of adolescent males. Here the adult world, if not entirely absent, is shown – disturbingly – to side with the worst elements among the boys in an American Catholic High School. Intimidation and persecution are the rule. The battle of the central figure, Jerry Renault, to endure bullying that is both ruthless and cunning has its climax in a boxing match at which the schoolboy spectators display a bloodlust that would not be inappropriate in a gladiatorial contest. The courage and isolated defiance of Jerry Renault don't earn the conventional rewards that we might expect in a piece of fiction. The book is uncomfortably close to real life. Like *Lord of the Flies*, *The Chocolate War* is pessimistic in its depiction of the human capacity for evil – or, at the least, of the evil of the few and the weakness of the majority. Tellingly, the last word of the novel is 'darkness'.

The conflict between good and evil may have a quality of grandeur, as in *Macbeth*, in its suggestion of fundamental and universal forces opposed to each other. On the other hand, the struggle can have a greyer, more routine aspect in which the very terms 'good' and 'evil' may seem over-dramatic. All the books referred to so far do, however, conceive of antagonistic impulses within the individual (child or adult) and draw their power from the war between those impulses. Each offers material for discussion or writing. An imaginative recreation of Macbeth's state of mind, for example, through the device of letters or diary entries written by him should make the student return to the text (always go back to the text!) for suggestions as to the turmoil of hopes and fears within this tragic figure. The novels by Golding and Cormier offer starting points for discussion on topics naturally relevant in adolescence, such as bullying, isolation, and conformity.

Divided loyalties

The texts discussed so far have centred on the conflict between good and evil originating within the individual and then emerging into the world outside. Most forms of inner conflict, however, do not take place on such a stark and dramatic battleground. We are unlikely to think of our predicaments as involving 'good' and 'evil' alternatives, but to use instead descriptions like 'divided loyalties', 'mixed feelings', and so on. It is usual to experience conflict over courses of action without 'right' and 'wrong' being involved. Many, perhaps most, of the everyday struggles will be between what we want to do and what we think other people want us to do. Such conflicts can be moralized in terms of 'selfishness' and 'duty', but the value given to these terms varies with the user and the context. To accuse someone of being 'selfish' is often a preliminary move in the campaign to get him or her to do what we want and may even be a means of concealing our own 'selfishness'. And if an individual is conducting such a debate with himself it's likely to be even more obscured by his own prejudices, delusions about himself, lack of objectivity, etc.

Great Expectations (1860–1)

Charles Dickens's *Great Expectations* provides a fine, gripping example of an individual at war with himself over just such issues. The novel is highly complex, and it must be emphasized that – as with *Macbeth* – to take the 'inner conflict' aspect is by no means to provide a full account of it. In *Great Expectations* we trace the progress, in a first person narrative, of Pip from boyhood to early middle age. Pip is an orphan, brought up by his unloving sister and her amiable but ineffectual husband, a village blacksmith. The novel, set in the early Victorian period, has a most dramatic opening, an encounter from which almost all the subsequent events in the narrative unfold, even though Pip does not understand this until near the end of the action.

Pip, a young child, alone in a churchyard gazing at the graves of his parents, is terrorized by an escaped convict who demands from the boy food and a file (to remove a fetter from his leg). Frightened at the prospect of stealing from his sister's house but even more frightened at the vengeance threatened by the convict if he doesn't produce the goods, Pip steals what is required and delivers everything to the hunted man. To little purpose, it seems, as he is recaptured later the same day, to be deported eventually to Australia. Years afterwards, when Pip has resigned himself to a dull life as an apprentice blacksmith in his brother-in-law's forge, Pip is given the wonderful news that he has a secret benefactor, someone who wants to give him a comfortable income and, more importantly, to fasten on him the status of a gentleman. To this end it is necessary that Pip move from home and install himself in London.

Pip's latent snobbery and dissatisfaction with his 'low' position as a 'common labouring boy' have already been stirred up by his encounters with the highly eccentric Miss Havisham and, more acutely, by the beautiful Estella, to whom Miss Havisham is guardian. Pip naturally enough assumes that the old lady is his anonymous benefactor, intent on training him up as a 'gentleman' to marry Estella. But the narrator has other ties than these. Though intimidated by his mean-minded sister, Pip has a real affection for Joe the blacksmith, as well as for Biddy, a village girl whose simplicity and modesty make her Estella's opposite. He is delighted to be leaving home and already considers himself several notches above his family. At the same time he feels guilty for feeling like this, and yet by a further twist cannot acknowledge the guilt for what it is. The following passage, just before Pip's departure for London, shows the confusion of thought and emotion. Pip is unwilling to exhibit himself in his new 'city' clothes to his unsophisticated neighbours:

English coursework: Conflict

'That's just what I don't want, Joe. They would make such a business of it – such a coarse and common business – that I couldn't bear myself.'

'Ah, that indeed, Pip!' said Joe. 'If you couldn't abear yourself—'

Biddy asked me here, as she sat holding my sister's plate, 'Have you thought about when you'll show yourself to Mr Gargery, and your sister, and me? You will show yourself to us; won't you?'

'Biddy,' I returned with some resentment, 'you are so exceedingly quick that it's difficult to keep up with you.' . . .

Biddy said no more. Handsomely forgiving her, I soon exchanged an affectionate good-night with her and Joe, and went up to bed . . .

The sun had been shining brightly all day on the roof of my attic, and the room was warm. As I put the window open and stood looking out, I saw Joe come slowly forth at the dark door below, and take a turn or two in the air; and then I saw Biddy come, and bring him a pipe and light it for him. He never smoked so late, and it seemed to hint to me that he wanted comforting, for some reason or other.

He presently stood at the door immediately beneath me, smoking his pipe, and Biddy stood there too, quietly talking to him, and I knew that they talked of me, for I heard my name mentioned in an endearing tone more than once. I would not have listened for more, if I could have heard more: so I drew away from the window, and sat down in my one chair by the bedside, feeling it very sorrowful and strange that this first night of my bright fortunes should be the loneliest I had ever known. (Chapter 18)

This passage registers Pip's distaste for his neighbours and surroundings – they are 'coarse' and 'common'. Guilt at feeling like this about the people and the place where he has grown up makes him defensive and ready to suspect criticism, as shown in his rebuke to Biddy. Pip finds himself excluded from the picture of domestic tranquillity which he spies on from his attic window ('I saw Biddy come, and bring him a pipe and light it for him'). More accurately, he has excluded himself from the scene by his air of superiority. He is lonely and, plainly, unhappy, but unable to see why. Incapable of understanding himself and suffering the effects of conflicting feelings, Pip equally lacks perception about others. Joe's smoking 'seemed to hint to me that he wanted comforting, for some reason or other'. Pip won't credit that Joe, who has been to him more like a brother than a figure of adult authority, is actually depressed at his friend's leaving for London; perhaps because to admit this in the privacy of his heart would be to intensify his misery.

The painful confusion of his emotions is a sign that his

Internal conflict

conscience (which 'tells' him that he should make a better return for Biddy and Joe's love of him) is pulling him in the opposite direction to a snobbish ambition (which 'tells' Pip that these are the kind of people he can't have much to do with in his new life). Dickens does not state this explicitly: since the story is seen through Pip's eyes what occurs in the narrative generally reflects his own incomplete or biased understanding.

In the last third of *Great Expectations* Pip discovers the identity of his secret benefactor: not Miss Havisham, but the convict Magwitch, who returns at the risk of his life from exile in Australia to see the boy he has transformed into a 'gentleman'. By a most poignant irony he has changed the child's handing over of food and the file in the churchyard years before, a 'crime' Pip committed from terror, into an act of charity by which a young boy showed pity to an outcast. At once the foundations of Pip's existence are smashed. His prosperity, his self-esteem, his remaining hopes of marrying Estella, all evaporate. Pip recoils from the convict – literally:

> The abhorrence in which I held the man, the dread I had of him, the repugnance with which I shrank from him, could not have been exceeded if he had been some terrible beast.
>
> 'Look'ee here, Pip. I'm your second father. You're my son – more to me nor any son. I've put away money, only for you to spend . . .'
> (Chapter 39)

Pip's knowledge that he owes his position to a common criminal is unendurable; he almost faints under the strain. Now a fresh conflict breaks out: between his abhorrence at Magwitch, a loathing that has strands of the physical, the social, and the moral in it, and his obligation towards a man who has devoted his life to enriching Pip's. And the adult Pip finds that this sense of obligation is as hard to remove as was once the fetter from the convict's leg. Finally a resolution of this conflict is achieved, and in arriving at it Pip reaches a quite different understanding of the term 'gentleman': not membership of a privileged class but possession of inward qualities; generosity, loyalty and the capacity to forgive.

An important component of Pip's debate with himself is his self-delusion. As suggested earlier, if we are 'arguing' with ourselves we find it difficult to set out the arguments clearly and impartially on each side of a question. We are prone to

English coursework: Conflict

manufacture reasons for following a particular course of action or to hide its disadvantages from ourselves: so Pip conceals from himself the full extent of his obligations towards Joe and Biddy because this makes his departure for London easier to manage.

Assignments

1 Turn the episode from *Great Expectations* where Pip is about to leave home into a page or two from a film (or television) script. How would you illustrate – by close-ups, camera angles, lighting, etc – Pip's confused state of mind? What have you gained and/or lost by transferring the episode from one medium to another?

2 Write about an occasion when, like Pip, you've been unhappy with yourself because of an inner conflict of impulses, between what you want to do and what you think you ought to do.

3 Which is more important, loyalty to oneself or loyalty to others? Find another text, such as *The Third Man* by Graham Greene, which deals with this issue.

Julius Caesar (1599)

Shakespeare, in *Julius Caesar*, gives us an interesting illustration of an individual who, after debating with himself, comes to the deluded conclusion that what he is doing is for the best. The individual is Brutus, the figurehead of the group of conspirators who stabbed Caesar in the senate in 44 BC. Brutus is renowned for his honour and integrity – at least in Shakespeare's characterization – and displays a subtle vanity about these traits in himself. The other conspirators know that Brutus's participation will transform them from mere murderers into noble benefactors of the Roman state. Because Caesar threatens to grow too powerful Brutus makes the decision to join the plot in this soliloquy:

> It must be by his death: and for my part,
> I know no personal cause to spurn at him,
> But for the general. He would be crown'd:
> How that might change his nature, there's the question:
> 5 It is the bright day that brings forth the adder,
> And that craves wary walking. Crown him? that;

> And then, I grant, we put a sting in him,
> That at his will he may do danger with.
> Th' abuse of greatness is when it disjoins
> 10 Remorse from power; and, to speak truth of Caesar,
> I have not know when his affections sway'd
> More than his reason. But 'tis a common proof,
> That lowliness is young ambition's ladder,
> Whereto the climber-upward turns his face;
> 15 But when he once obtains the upmost round,
> He then unto the ladder turns his back,
> Looks in the clouds, scorning the base degrees
> By which he did ascend. So Caesar may:
> Then lest he may, prevent. And since the quarrel
> 20 Will bear no colour for the thing he is,
> Fashion it thus: that what he is, augmented,
> Would run to these and these extremities;
> And therefore think him as a serpent's egg,
> Which, hatch'd, would, as his kind, grow mischievous,
> 25 And kill him in the shell. (II,1)

Read the speech carefully. Check the sense of any words you don't understand. Remember that these are the words of a man choosing to commit a murder, for the best reasons – as he sees it. At one level the lines are clear, relatively unemotional. The speech seems to lack the signs of inner conflict. But in fact Brutus is doing a clever job of persuading himself into the killing of Julius Caesar. This is difficult because he has no personal motive for wanting Caesar out of the way, and he has no evidence that the other man will abuse his power if he is crowned Emperor. For a variety of reasons, however, one of which is certainly vanity, Brutus wishes to take part in the conspiracy.

He must therefore argue against his personal knowledge of a man who is a friend: 'I have not known when his affections sway'd/More than his reason' (11–12); i.e. Caesar has never let his feelings dominate his cooler judgement. He has to retreat into generalization ("tis a common proof..."): ambitious people stamp on those who have helped them to the top. He has to search for proverbial reassurance: 'It is the bright day that brings forth the adder' (5). Caesar is snakelike: harmless when unhatched but venomous when free of his shell and basking in the sun, the power and glory of being Emperor (23–5).

The clarity of the speech is deceptive. It appears to be honest, as when Brutus concedes that he has no personal motive for killing Caesar (1-3), or that Caesar's present behaviour gives no pretext for such an act. This honesty seems to heighten the 'selfless' quality of what Brutus proposes: it must be a proper action, because he himself will get nothing out of it. It is 'for the general [good]' (3). But the honesty is questionable. Brutus is like a man who plays the part of a prosecutor bringing a case against one who has committed no crime, and then, not yet content, assumes the authority of a judge as he condemns the accused to death because of what he *might* still do (18-25).

At the same time as the honesty underlines Caesar's 'innocence' it also, self-servingly, confirms Brutus in his own eyes as a man of integrity who will not deceive himself. Yet he does deceive himself into thinking that a murder is required, and Shakespeare remorselessly shows how the assassination, far from serving the public good, plunges Rome into civil war. Brutus stands convicted, by the drama as a whole, of political naïvety and arrogant high-mindedness, as he persuades himself that a 'selfless' action is in addition a 'noble' one – even if it's murder.

The conflict in this scene is therefore of a subtler kind. A combination of vanity and a sense of public obligation draw Brutus into the conspiracy; these, and especially the latter, are powerful enough to turn murder into sacrifice. Brutus can give the conspirators the elevated status of priests carrying out a ritual slaughter; they are protected and sanctified by what they are doing (see his other speeches in II,1). On the other side is Brutus's natural distaste at the killing, for he is not a ruthless or bloodthirsty man; but, as irrevocably as Macbeth, Brutus discovers himself committed to a bloody course that will terminate only with his own death. The difference is that Macbeth has consciously chosen evil, while Brutus believes himself to be doing good. Each man has in common that he has been the victim of conflicting impulses, chosen the wrong course, and suffered for it. In *Julius Caesar*, however, good and evil are not in question. Here we are in a political world in which actions are expedient rather than moral; ultimate victory goes not to the 'good' but to forces that are more powerful, cunning or ruthless than their opposition.

Huckleberry Finn (1885)

One further example of the war between conflicting impulses, and involving a kind of self-deception, will be given. This is from *The Adventures of Huckleberry Finn* by Mark Twain, whose boy-hero spends much of the narrative sailing on a raft down the Mississippi in the company of a runaway slave. At one point Huck thinks that it's his duty to hand the negro Jim back to his owner. That he is really unwilling to do so he takes as evidence of his own corrupt and sinful nature:

Well, I tried the best I could to kinder soften it up somehow for myself, by saying I was brung up wicked, and so I warn't so much to blame; but something inside of me kept saying, 'There was the Sunday school, you could a gone to it; and if you'd a done it they'd a learnt you, there, that people that acts as I'd been acting about that nigger goes to everlasting fire.' (Chapter 31)

Eventually Huck steels himself to write a note revealing Jim's whereabouts, and immediately, 'I felt good and all washed clean of sin for the first time I had ever felt so in my life . . .' Then he recollects how close he and Jim had been on their voyage and how the black man said Huck 'was the best friend old Jim ever had in the world'. The boy is torn between the generous desire to protect a friend and the cold impulse of 'conscience' which informs him that a runaway slave is a criminal who deserves to be turned in. He has to decide, as he gazes at the treacherous note he has written:

'All right, then, I'll *go* to hell' and tore it up.
It was awful thoughts, and awful words, but they was said. And I let them stay said; and never thought no more about reforming. I shoved the whole thing out of my head; and said I would take up wickedness again, which was in my line, being brung up to it, and the other warn't.

From the reader's point of view the 'right' impulse wins here. But Huck feels it to be the wrong one: he is going against the social code that says an escaped slave is no more than a piece of property. Twain's irony makes Huck's 'wrong' right, and his notion of 'right' wrong. Huck's 'conscience' is a false one, twisted by exposure to a society that is not properly civilized (because it treats one group of people as objects). The novel demonstrates how he overcomes the promptings of this false conscience and learns to listen to the liberating instincts that transform Jim from runaway to friend.

It may be observed that the element of self-deception in Huck's argument with himself is different from that encountered in the examples drawn from *Julius Caesar* and *Great Expectations*. Pip's snobbery and ambition blind him to aspects of himself and of those around him; Brutus's self-deluded musings on public responsibility dignify murder and cause him to take a wild leap into the dark (for he has no idea at all of what will follow on the death of Caesar). Huckleberry Finn, on the other hand, is 'tricked' by a set of false values imposed from outside and only partially absorbed; but these are civilized lessons that he has – fortunately – never taken properly to heart, and his innate generosity wins the battle.

From this discussion it should be apparent that this form of inner conflict, in which emotion and reason are powerfully but (often) obscurely at work and in which there is no obvious 'right' course, is perhaps the most subtle of all forms of inner debate. When we come across instances of it, in drama, in prose narrative, we must assess not merely a character's motives as he declares them but search also for what he does *not* say. In addition, we must assess a character's assessment of himself. Is Brutus really the selfless public servant he considers himself? Why is Huck Finn wrong to accuse himself of 'wickedness', and what does that accusation tell us about the civilization he wants to escape from?

Questions of life and death

There is another type of inner debate in which the issues are more clear-cut, or are presented as such to the participants. As examples take two twentieth-century plays, both with historical settings and both dealing with the conflict between conscience and the natural desire for self-preservation. The central characters here aren't in any doubt about the choice open to them. Their eyes are open, and there is no self-deception. *The Crucible* (1952) by Arthur Miller and *A Man for All Seasons* (1960) by Robert Bolt focus on the dilemma confronted by their protagonists, a dilemma involving the penalty (death) for staying loyal to one's inner conscience and principles, and the reward (being allowed to live) for abandoning them. Both plays contain exciting court-room scenes: there is, on a basic level, a theatrical quality to the costumes worn by some of the 'players' (wigs, gowns), there is an inbuilt conflict since every trial necessitates confrontation, there is the added thrill that an individual's reputation, freedom, even life, may be lost.

The Crucible (1952) and A Man for All Seasons (1960)

It is life that is at risk for John Proctor, the central figure in *The Crucible*. Falsely accused of witchcraft – the play is based on the witch-hunting hysteria that seized Salem, Massachusetts, in the late seventeenth century – Proctor must decide whether to sign his name to a false confession and thus save his life. The alternative is to save his name – by going to the gallows. Such a bare summary does very little justice to the emotional complexity and intensity of the conclusion to the play, but the relevant point is that the conflict is entirely internal, since no one can take Proctor's decision for him, literally a matter of life and death. A parallel dilemma confronts Thomas More in Bolt's *A Man for All Seasons*. More was Chancellor to Henry VIII until he was stripped of his office and eventually imprisoned because of his disagreement with the King over the latter's remarriage. Again, the issues involved are complex, but the case comes down to More's swearing an oath (to the Act of Succession) in violation of his conscience, or keeping silent, and being tried for treason. More elects to stay silent, just as Proctor elects not to sign. Both are actions that are, more properly, denials of action. Heroism lies in non-cooperation, although neither man looks to be a hero.

There is a revealing similarity in the way each individual talks about the critical choice confronting him. Taking an oath is for Thomas More an utterly serious matter. He says to his daughter:

When a man takes an oath, Meg, he's holding his own self in his own hands. Like water [*cups hands*] and if he opens his fingers *then* – he needn't hope to find himself again.

For John Proctor to sign his name to a false document is to abandon the only thing he has left. When the demand is made of him – why will he not add his signature? – he cries out:

Because it is my name! Because I cannot have another in my life! Because I lie and sign myself to lies! . . . How may I live without my name?

In each instance the central character is driven, desperately and unwillingly, to a defence of his 'name'; that which represents for him a mark of irreducible individuality. Both would be lost and no longer themselves, without their names. To give them away, in speech or writing, is to surrender everything. For this they are prepared to go to their deaths.

The Crucible and *A Man for All Seasons* present a dignified, elevated view of the heroism of two men for whom life is liveable only if they are enabled to retain some self-respect. Although Proctor and More are shown in conflict with hostile, morally unworthy societies, it is on their battles with themselves that the dramatists concentrate. It might be added that the two opposed elements in this inner conflict – self-preservation and conscience – present particular difficulties of interpretation for an audience, and are intended to do so. Neither More nor Proctor would harm anybody else by giving in and signing or swearing to something they didn't believe in. In fact they heap misery on their families and friends by persisting in a course that leads to martyrdom. In saving themselves they would not only be obeying a universal instinct (of self-preservation) but acting in a manner that would earn them widespread approval. As we watch or read these plays we are meant to sympathize with the arguments and dilemmas of the protagonists as well as the sincere pleas of those who attempt to make these brave men change their convictions.

Love versus duty

An obvious variant on the topic of 'conscience versus self-preservation' is the conflict between love and duty. Shakespeare's *Antony and Cleopatra* deals with just this subject. So, on a less subtle but still engrossing level, does *Jane Eyre* by Charlotte Brontë.

Jane Eyre (1847)

This is one of the most famous of romantic novels, although alongside the 'Cinderella' component of the story is an interesting examination of the status of women in a male-dominated society. (For a more detailed analysis refer to the Brodie's Note on *Women and Society*.) Jane Eyre, a governess, is proposed to by the stern and enigmatic Mr Rochester. As the couple are at the altar the ceremony is interrupted by a stranger, who reveals that the bridegroom 'has a wife now living'. Rochester's wife is mad, confined to an upper floor in his mansion. After the shock of the revelation has faded – the wedding, of course, can't take place – Rochester urges Jane to remain with him. She is tempted but in the end follows her conscience and leaves the man who can never be her husband:

> He turned away; he threw himself on his face on the sofa. 'Oh Jane! my hope – my love – my life!' broke in anguish from his lips. Then came a deep, strong sob.
> I had already gained the door; but, reader, I walked back – walked back as determinedly as I had retreated. I knelt down by him; I turned his face from the cushion to me; I kissed his cheek; I smoothed his hair with my hand.
> 'God bless you, my dear master!' I said. 'God keep you from harm and wrong – direct you, solace you – reward you well for your past kindness to me.'
> 'Little Jane's love would have been my best reward,' he answered; 'without it, my heart is broken. But Jane will give me her love; yes – nobly, generously.' (Chapter 27)

Jane may give him her love, but she won't stay. She appears in perfect control of herself here. Charlotte Brontë, however, conveys to us elsewhere the complexity of the situation and does not gloss over the tensions and inner conflict that she experiences.

Conscience, for the heroine, can cut two ways. Before she departs Rochester explains how he came to marry, and how subsequently he came to fall in love with Jane. He throws himself on her mercy:

> 'Is it better to drive a fellow-creature to despair than to transgress a mere human law, no man being injured by the breach? – for you have neither relatives nor acquaintances whom you need fear to offend by living with me?'
> This was true: and while he spoke my very conscience and reason turned traitors against me, and charged me with crime in resisting him. They spoke almost as loud as Feeling: and that clamoured wildly. 'Oh, comply!' it said.

Almost everything is stacked against her. Not only does she have Rochester's compelling voice begging her to stay, she is urged by her own inner instincts to the same course. Reason informs her that Rochester is right; conscience makes her afraid of what he might do to himself if she goes; above all, feeling (which 'clamoured wildly') pulls her. In addition Rochester has made it clear earlier in their conversation that he doesn't intend her to be his mistress if she agrees to live with him. That he is prepared to forgo any sexual demand so as to win her consent to their staying together gives to his love a platonic and selfless quality. It's an indication of his devotion, and a further pressure on the heroine. Nevertheless, a stern morality drives Jane from his house. Jane is not governed only by the cold 'laws and principles' which she refers to in debate with herself; self-respect is also involved. To remain with Rochester would, in some sense, be an abandonment of self.

It hardly needs to be said that this is not the conclusion to *Jane Eyre*. A classic – and happy – love story cannot end with a parting. But by the end Charlotte Brontë has so arranged her narrative that conflicting demands, for justice and for a romantically fitting conclusion, can be satisfied. Morality and romance are compatible.

To summarize the different areas of inner conflict examined in this section: there was first the most extreme clash, between good and evil, embodied in the person of Macbeth. The same conflict is dramatized in texts such as *Dr Jekyll and Mr Hyde* and *Lord of the Flies*. After that we come to a less clearly defined region in which concepts such as self-interest, conscience, love, duty, self-deception will exert pressure or hold out enticements to the individual. Here it is important to note that right and wrong, if involved at all, may be hard to discern. As we have seen, Huckleberry Finn's concept of 'right' would lead to his betraying a runaway slave, while Brutus's notion that he is acting rightly in his country's interest leads to a civil war. For Jane Eyre there is right on both sides – and the reader must appreciate this if he or she is fully receptive to the novel. Morality and self-esteem direct her away from the man she loves, compassion draws her back again. Conscience is operating on both sides, and, unlike in *Huckleberry Finn*, it is not possible to claim that one of these 'consciences' is false or should be ignored.

Careful examination of these and other texts which provide instances of inner conflict – and you must of course search for additional examples and references to those already quoted – should show that when a character in a novel or a play is in 'debate' with himself, all kinds of factors are at work. And if we try to look at ourselves honestly when embroiled in some inner 'argument' then we will find the same.

External conflict

General introduction

The movement of this discussion of conflict is from inner to outer, beginning with the individual and finishing with a short treatment of the theme as it appears in stories and poems concerned with conflict in its ultimate form: war. However it should be appreciated that there is no clear distinction between the 'inner' and the 'outer'. What we think and feel will determine what we do – or don't do. Even a completely unresolved situation of conflict, resulting in indecision or inaction, will manifest itself in some shape in the outside world. And a person suffering from confusion or tension within himself is more than likely to demonstrate it unawares. When Macbeth first hears the witches' prophecies he becomes 'rapt' (absolutely absorbed by his own thoughts) and his companions notice this. Later his wife tells him that his looks betray him: his face 'is as a book where men/May read strange matters'. Pip, in *Great Expectations*, cannot help recoiling from the convict Magwitch, although his consciousness of how much he owes to the man, and the other's evident delight at seeing him, prevent him from actually saying the words that would convey his loathing.

An inner conflict, therefore, will be signified by gesture, expression, strained behaviour of some sort, unless the person experiencing it is very self-disciplined. Shakespeare gives us an insight into the psychological cost of such 'self-discipline' in the character of Lady Macbeth. She is calm about what they are doing; she has to be, to coax her husband into murder, and we see her as heartless and guiltless. When Duncan has been killed in his sleep, and Macbeth is in a condition of near hysteria, she takes command, returns the murder weapons to Duncan's bedchamber, comes back and upbraids Macbeth for his cowardice: 'My hands are of your colour, but I shame/To wear a heart so white.' For her, murder is something that can be washed away; you must use water to clean the bloodstains from your hands, but your conscience requires no cleansing – either because it's non-existent or, as in the case of Lady Macbeth, because it has been suppressed. For two-thirds of the play Lady Macbeth acts as a cool, self-possessed contrast to her husband. Then she disappears from the scene while he persists in his murderous progress. By a daring imaginative leap – daring, because he has provided no interim moments of explanation – Shakespeare has her emerge (at the beginning of Act V), maddened by the knowledge of what she and her husband have performed together. We understand that she has paid as heavy a price as her husband; perhaps a heavier one. The appearance of a character committed to evil but at peace with herself is illusory. The conflict within her is all the more violent when it finally manifests itself, because it has for so long been so rigorously suppressed.

What is inward eventually becomes outward. The battle inside Macbeth becomes battle on the soil of Scotland: the divisions in Brutus as he argues himself into an assassination are amplified into the divisions of the civil war which overtakes the Roman state. It is of the nature of conflict that it is not static for long: one side or the other will eventually predominate. Either the struggle will be resolved 'peacefully' (as Pip at last resolves his opposing feelings about Magwitch and comes to love his benefactor), or it will terminate in a genuine battle – of anything from words to weapons – in the outside world. But the consequences of inner turmoil will always be felt in the world, whether those consequences are destructive or benign.

The various sorts of conflict touched on in this study cannot therefore be rigidly compartmentalized. To take an example from a text already discussed, *The Crucible*: Arthur Miller's central character is John Proctor, the 'average' man driven to a final desperate defence of self. But Proctor is only part of a larger canvas in which the individual is set against the community, and in which there is dissension in each of the varied groupings which comprise it. Conflict operates at all levels.

Group conflict: family and class

A gentle introduction to the subject in a broader context is provided by the poem 'Digging' by the Irish writer, Seamus Heaney. Here the writer, who comes from a farming community in Northern Ireland, feels an apparent sense of guilt that he has relinquished the traditional agricultural occupations of his father and his grandfather. They were men skilled with their hands (harvesting the potato crop, digging up blocks of turf). Heaney is also skilled – with a pen, the writer's implement. The pen is described at the beginning of the poem as sitting 'snug as a gun' in his hand. By the end of the poem Heaney has come to terms with his feelings, and his family. As his predecessors dug into the earth, so he too will 'dig', but not in a literal sense. He will use a pen rather than a spade. We may imagine some of the ways in which a writer might dig, into his past, into his self, and bring to the surface the crop that has been growing in secret.

The poem, a good introduction to Heaney's difficult but rewarding work, confers dignity both on his chosen occupation and that of his forefathers. Different generations are aligned by the use of imagery: the pen, a threatening 'gun' at the start, becomes by the conclusion a 'spade', something more pacific and creative. It would be correct to say that there is an inner conflict in these lines – Heaney is plainly uncomfortable with himself, and that has stimulated him into writing – but implicit here is a family conflict. Heaney feels himself at odds with men whom he respects, and can only afford to relax after he's persuaded himself that his job isn't so very different, after all, from theirs. A similar sense of family discomfort is evident in 'Follower', another poem from the same early collection, *Death of a Naturalist* (1966).

The family is a plausible arena for conflict. Differing aspirations, envy and jealousy, issues of authority and dependence – all are likely to be found in the close community of a family and all are likely to cause friction. One of the draws of writing about the family for a novelist, poet or dramatist is that the interplay between the members of this group will be both intense and familiar to readers or audience. In addition, for the serious writer, dealing with the question of the 'family' in artistic terms may well be a means of reconciling himself to troubling or baffling aspects of his own life.

Sons and Lovers (1913) and *The Daughter-in-Law (c.1913)*

D. H. Lawrence used one of his earlier novels as a means of coming to terms with his parents and his past. By recreating situations of fundamental conflict, he was trying to distance and put under artistic control his own painful memories. *Sons and Lovers* handles the early life of Paul Morel, a figure modelled on

Lawrence himself. He goes back well before the birth of his protagonist to show the first meeting of Paul's parents, and how they are mutually attracted by their differences; the future Mrs Morel is more 'refined' than her coal-miner husband. Disappointed at him in the early days of their marriage, Mrs Morel turns the fire of her love and displaced ambition on her sons. After the premature death of William, she grows more fiercely possessive of Paul, and the greater part of *Sons and Lovers* charts their painful, anxious relationship, painful especially when Paul becomes involved with two other women, one virginal, the other worldly. The novel, very scantly summarized here, closes after the protracted and anguished death of Mrs Morel, and it would be more accurate to claim that this produces in Paul not so much a resolution of his inner conflict but a purged state in which he is incapable of feeling anything but exhaustion.

The title *Sons and Lovers* suggests the dual roles that Paul Morel is obliged to play, and the very balance hints at his suspended state, his inability to fix himself as son *or* lover (or prospective husband). At about the same period Lawrence wrote *The Daughter-in-Law*, a play that deals with some of the same issues of jealousy and independence. Luther Gascoigne is a miner; in the first act he learns that he has made a girl pregnant. He has however very recently married Minnie, who (like Mrs Morel) is slightly above her husband socially. The marriage is already on the rocks, and Minnie has little hesitation in pinning the blame not on her husband but on her mother-in-law. She identifies her rival, the 'other woman', not as the pregnant girl but as Mrs Gascoigne:

MINNIE: You didn't care what women your sons went with, so long as they didn't love them. What do you care really about this affair of Bertha Purdy? You don't. All you cared about was to keep your sons for yourself. You kept the solid meal, and the orts and slarts any other woman could have. But I tell you, I'm *not* for having the orts and slarts, and your leavings from your sons. I'll have a man, or nothing, I will.
MRS GASCOIGNE: It's rare to be some folks, ter pick and choose.
MINNIE: I can't pick and choose, no. But what I won't have, I won't have, and that is all.
MRS GASCOIGNE [to LUTHER]: Have I ever kept thee from doin' as tha wanted? Have I iver marded and coddled thee?
LUTHER: Tha hasna, beguy!
MINNIE: No, you haven't, perhaps, not by the look of things. But you've

bossed him. You've decided everything for him, really. He's depended on you as much when he was thirty as when he was three. You told him what to do, and he did it.

The conflict here is over 'possession'. Minnie regards herself as not having a true husband because he is still in a sense the 'property' of his mother, and happy to be so: he's never really grown up. It would be a worthwhile exercise to make an extended comparison of Lawrence's novel and play. Both are concerned with the triangle of son-mother-'other woman'. As the title of the play suggests, Lawrence examines the problem here as much from the point of view of the 'outsider' as from that of the son or the mother. *The Daughter-in-Law* is a slighter but warmer and less introspective work than *Sons and Lovers* and one in which Lawrence gains a more objective grasp on his experience.

It has already been indicated that one reason for the friction between husband and wife in both novel and play is the small difference in class between them. This is shown by the short excerpt from *The Daughter-in-Law*: Luther Gascoigne and his mother speak in (Nottinghamshire) dialect while the better educated Minnie's speech conforms to 'standard English'. Speech signifies class. Dialect, accent, choice of words, all enable a reader or audience to bracket a character somewhere on the social spectrum. More generally, class conflict is a fertile subject for writers and though not necessarily occupying a central place in a novel or a drama – as, say, racial conflict will – it may nevertheless contribute towards an intensification of atmosphere where the root cause of the conflict may be something different. This is the case with the two works by Lawrence referred to.

An Inspector Calls (1947)

Class is certainly a feature of J. B. Priestley's drama *An Inspector Calls*, which dramatizes an investigation into the death of a girl at the hands of a prosperous, complacent, middle-class family in a Midlands city. The play was first performed just after the Second World War but is set in the period before 1914. One of the twists in the ingenious plot is that none of the members of the Birling family appears to have actually committed a 'crime'.

But, the Inspector insists, the girl has taken her own life because of the collective selfishness and carelessness of the family, and the less insensitive among them gradually come to realize that he is right. They are all guilty. The girl died because she was not of their class and therefore didn't deserve their attention. To the factory-owning Mr Birling she was merely cheap labour; to his daughter an arrogant and impertinent shop girl and to her fiancé an unremarkable mistress, to his son a casual affair and a bought-off pregnancy, to his wife a woman undeserving of charity. Priestley sees the relationship between the classes as being that between persecutor and victim. Eva Smith, the working girl, has been moral and restrained in her dealings with the Birling family; they are exposed as weaklings or hypocrites, lacking her courage and doubly damned because of the privileged positions which they fill. The simplicity of this opposition makes for a satisfying if straightforward drama.

A Kind of Loving (1960)

The novels and plays discussed in this section come, by and large, under the heading of 'realist' work; that is, they present a familiar or persuasive picture of everyday life, accurate in its surface detail. It is to be expected that family or class conflict will surface in this kind of writing. Most of us, after all, aren't confronted with the possibility of murdering a king or a would-be dictator (*Macbeth*, *Julius Caesar*). Few of us will have to encounter a convict who demanded food from us as children. But almost all of us will have to deal with struggles and conflicts arising from our status as members of families or social groupings. These are familiar battles. They demand, perhaps, a more realistic and matter of fact treatment than that given to more heroic or obviously dramatic types of conflict.

In the 1950s and 1960s there was a vogue for plays and novels that dealt in 'realistic' terms with conflict within families or between classes. It was a period in which old certainties seemed to be dissolving, in which class boundaries were more acutely felt but were also perceived as being easier to cross. Well-known plays such as *Look Back in Anger* (1957) by John Osborne, and various novels of the period, such as *Saturday Night and Sunday Morning* (1958) by Alan Sillitoe, conveyed a sense of frustration and impatience with the traditional order of things, a feeling that the old and established members of society had too much of everything and that the rest – the young, the working-class – had too little.

One of the most sensitive and readable works of this time is Stan Barstow's *A Kind of Loving*. Its interest comes not only from the honest and unpretentious character of its first person narrator, Vic Brown, but also from the fact that the story is set in a period of social transition. Vic falls in love with a woman who works at his office. Eventually he grows disenchanted with her but her pregnancy commits him to marriage. The expectations of the two families concerned, the prevailing moral climate, and above all Vic's own concept of decency push him into a union which he doesn't want – he describes it as if he is starting a prison sentence – but which he cannot honourably avoid. *A Kind of Loving* can be studied for examples of various sorts of conflict, from the inner – Vic has fierce disputes with himself at each stage of his relationship with Ingrid – to the external. There is sexual conflict, family debate, class friction. When Vic is 'interviewed' by his prospective parents-in-law the experience is a painful one. He is loaded with guilt and too downcast to react to Mrs Rothwell's snobbish assumption of social superiority.

> 'How long have you known my daughter?' she says now, like a duchess asking a gardener for his references. I nearly expect her to say 'Brown', but she doesn't call me by any name all evening.
> 'Well we've known one another by sight for a long time, but we've been friendly about eighteen months.'
> 'Friendly!' she says, screwing her little mouth up. 'I suppose you realize that this business has upset Ingrid's father and I very much.'
> 'I suppose it must have. It's only natural.' I try to look shame-faced and it's not so hard because I'm feeling that miserable. (Part Two, chapter 5)

The antagonism between the two is obvious, and it is based in part on social difference. Vic feels patronized by Mrs Rothwell – she talks to him 'like a duchess'. Like D. H. Lawrence in *The Daughter-in-Law* Barstow uses language to indicate class distinction. Vic's parents talk differently from Ingrid's, although the author signals by Mrs Rothwell's slightly shaky grammar ('... this business has upset Ingrid's father and I ...') her desperate need to assert her gentility to prove that they are better (morally, socially) than the hapless Vic.

English coursework: Conflict

A useful exercise in considering this aspect of conflict would be to take a passage of dialogue from a drama or a story, and discuss what each character's use of language suggests about his/her feelings at that stage in the action. Look at the choice of words and their arrangement. Is this character trying to impress? Is he in control of his emotions? Is she being as frank as she appears, or is something held back? Try to describe the tone of each side in an argument: self-righteous, defensive, calm, assertive, and so on. It is quite possible to interpret a stretch of dialogue in various ways. Consider the many tones in which the barest monosyllable – 'Yes', 'No' – can be delivered, and then extend that understanding to longer exchanges. Look too at the interplay between characters in a story, particularly where the conflict is heated and confined, as in a dispute involving family or one with class overtones. Observe how the way one person makes a statement or asks a question modifies the manner in which the other speaker replies.

Assignments

1 Some reasons why the family can turn into a battleground are briefly indicated above – conflicting ambitions, envy, etc. Write about one such battle in any text (such as *Spring and Port Wine*) which you have read and explain how the conflict has arisen.

2 What in your view are the things that most often cause conflict within the family?

3 Read the poem 'Follower' by Seamus Heaney. At the beginning the writer feels admiration for his father, but by the end his feelings aren't so clear-cut. Why is this? Discuss the way Heaney uses language to show the change.

4 Find a scene involving family conflict in any of the texts discussed in this section (or any other suitable book). Turn it into a play scene (if from a novel) or into a couple of pages from a novel (if from a play), with appropriate directions and descriptions. What would make the scene turn out differently?

Group conflict: race and culture

As we move outward to examine the theme of conflict on a wider scale it is worth noting that each level of conflict can absorb, as it were, the one beneath. Individuals in a family may quarrel bitterly but are quite likely to come together if faced by threat or even criticism. An endangered community will probably act as one although, in normal times, it may be made up of many wrangling factions. Small differences disappear, or are set aside, when the safety or reputation of the group is at stake. A nation at war is likely to enjoy a sense of unity – or at least the appearance of it – greater than it will ever achieve in peacetime. In the unifying process, however, what will be lost is the individual.

So it is when we examine religious and racial conflict. These involve people in the mass, people who are all assumed to be marching under the same banner of belief or colour. The thing that matters here is sameness: one member of a religious or racial group is assumed to be similar, even identical, to any other member of the group. But the novelist or dramatist works essentially with *individuals*, even if those individuals represent larger forces outside themselves. Paradoxically, the greater the scale of the conflict the more the writer needs to focus on the particular, the individual, in order to achieve a satisfactory realization of the material. This is especially true of literature that deals with full-scale war, as we shall see later in this study, but it applies too to texts that handle the important issues of religious, racial and cultural conflict.

Broadly speaking, it is possible to identify at least two methods of approaching the topic of conflict on this larger canvas. There are works that show up the existence of prejudice – racial, cultural, religious – so as to condemn it. And there are texts that, more neutrally, depict opposed cultures without suggesting that there is anything necessarily unhealthy or undesirable in such an opposition. In this latter type our notion of conflict will have to be modified.

To Kill a Mockingbird (1960)

The first example discussed here, however, is of the kind that attacks prejudice, albeit in a subtle fashion. Harper Lee's famous novel is set in the 1930s, a period when the low status of the black minorities in the southern states of America went largely unquestioned. The story is narrated by Scout Finch, the young daughter of a widowed Alabaman lawyer. She and her brother have to confront the anger and insults of many of the inhabitants of their small town when Atticus Finch agrees to defend a black man against a rape charge. The general supposition is that the negro is guilty because two white people say he is – even though it is plain to the reader (as it would be to any unbiased observer) that the whites are lying and that other evidence against the accused does not stand up to examination. The novel is a call for justice and tolerance. It is also a warning, for, says Atticus the lawyer, injustice and prejudice will eventually recoil on the whites: 'Don't fool yourselves – it's all adding up, and one of these days we're going to pay the bill for it. I hope it's not in your children's time.'

Such direct statement is untypical of the novel as a whole. *To Kill a Mockingbird* is not a sermon or a lecture on the requirement that one group behave well towards another. The plea for tolerance is implicit in the narrative and the book extends to an examination of prejudice beyond the simply racial. Scout and Jem, her brother, come to realize that their view of some of their fellow townspeople is wrong, most notably in the case of Boo Radley, a neighbour to whom all sorts of fears and superstitions are attached. Behind the mask, beneath the frightening manner, are human faces. It is a gentle and reassuring discovery. Indeed the words apply to the tone of the book as a whole, although the brutal and destructive effect of racial prejudice is acknowledged in full and there are aspects of tragedy to its conclusion. Harper Lee offers a kind of tolerance even to her most intolerant characters – or rather Atticus Finch does, as he points out to his children the redeeming features of even the most mean-minded or blinkered of the town's inhabitants. Open-eyed and unsentimental, yet generous in approach – this, together with its precise evocation of childhood in the pre-war American South, helps to account for the appeal and success of the narrative.

The Merchant of Venice (1596–7)

If we step back several centuries we discover a different type of racial (and religious) prejudice on display, and one where it is much harder to gauge the author's intentions. Shakespeare's *Merchant of Venice* has already been referred to in the introduction as presenting to its audience a character – Shylock, the Jewish money-lender – who is in conflict with himself, and who raises incompatible reactions in us; reactions which may range from pity to dislike, even revulsion.

Shylock is an outcast. He returns the hate that he receives because of his race and because of the way he earns his living. An instance of his capacity to hate is given when he says of Antonio (the Merchant of the title):

> I hate him for he is a Christian:
> But more, for that in low simplicity
> He lends out money gratis, and brings down
> The rate of usance here with us in Venice.
> 5 If I can catch him once upon the hip,
> I will feed fat the ancient grudge I bear him.
> He hates our sacred nation, and he rails
> (Even there where merchants most do congregate)
> On me, my bargains, and my well-won thrift,
> 10 Which he calls interest: cursed be my tribe
> If I forgive him! (I,3)

gratis: *without charging interest*

Racial prejudice is here reciprocated. Shylock is not a passive victim, but, given the chance, an aggressive tormentor. *The Merchant of Venice* makes a modern audience uncomfortable. The consequences of antisemitism in this century have been so appalling that to permit a display of it – or, as here, have a persecuted man profess hatred and vengeance – without some corrective commentary from the author, as Harper Lee subtly but insistently shows in *To Kill a Mockingbird* that racial prejudice is foolish and dangerous, is to risk being condemned. The excerpt already given in the introduction shows Shylock asserting his common humanity with Christians, but doing so in a troubling way: he is sufficiently like them to want to take revenge if wronged. His comments imply that he is neither better nor worse than members of the opposing religion and race, and there is in his words an implied criticism of Christian society which is valid irrespective of the speaker: the point that many Christians don't behave with the restraint they preach.

Shakespeare plainly demonstrates the kind of abuse to which Shylock is subject. Antonio, who has come to borrow, has no intention of softening his attitude towards the money-lender:

> I am as like to call thee so [dog] again,
> To spet on thee again, to spurn thee too. (I,3)

Shylock has accumulated a heap of complaints against this particular Christian merchant. The famous 'I am a Jew' speech begins: 'He hath disgrac'd me ... laugh'd at my losses, mock'd at my gains ... cooled my friends, heated mine enemies ...' (III,1). There are additional factors. His daughter has eloped with a Christian, taking with her the ring given to Shylock by his late wife before they married. She has exchanged the ring for a monkey, provoking in Shylock the tortured cry:

> It was my turquoise; I had it of Leah when I was a bachelor: I would not have given it for a wilderness of monkeys.

Shylock's expressions of anguish outdo those of any other character in the play, and yet Shakespeare doesn't let us feel a straightforward pity. Shylock, bitter, obsessively vindictive over his 'pound of flesh', insisting that the letter of the law be applied to his enemy, and closing his ears to all appeals to leniency, including Portia's well-known lines beginning 'The quality of mercy is not strained', cannot escape the logical outcome of his demand for absolute justice and our reaction is appropriately compromised.

In this clash of races and religions it is Shylock who loses. He forfeits half his property and his right to practise his faith, for it is part of the court's judgement that he 'become a Christian'. The unease we feel at this forced 'conversion' would not have been experienced by Shakespeare's audience. Rather, it would have been perceived as the Jew as being saved from damnation. But our reaction highlights the remorseless quality of racial conflict. In *The Merchant of Venice* there is either a suspicious coexistence between the two groups or, as at the end, the compulsory assimilation of a member of one group into the larger, dominant sect.

On the Black Hill (1982) and Things Fall Apart (1958)

Two modern texts offer fascinating examples of clashes between cultures and races. One suggests that the clash is ultimately benign as well as inevitable, the other shows the collision as merely inevitable. Bruce Chatwin's *On the Black Hill* gives a panoramic view of the history of this century as seen from a very local standpoint. The novel concerns itself with the lives of twins (born in 1900) to a Welsh father and an English mother. Lewis and Benjamin are inseparable. Though temperamentally different, they stay life-long partners in a manner that recalls the difficult but enduring relationship of their parents (the opening sentence of the novel is: 'For forty-two years, Lewis and Benjamin Jones slept side by side, in their parents' bed, at their farm which was known as "The Vision".'). The dominant idea of *On the Black Hill* is that relationships – between husband and wife, members of a family, varied cultures, even nations – may be the stronger precisely because of difference and conflict. Such a relationship is complementary. As twins, Lewis and Benjamin share an intimacy which is already durable and mysterious. Bruce Chatwin gives to each 'half' of the partnership opposed qualities: to Lewis a (traditionally) masculine vigour, for we are told that even at eighty he 'could walk over the hills all day, or wield an axe all day, and not get tired'; to Benjamin the (traditionally) feminine qualities of the home-maker: 'He did all the cooking, the darning and the ironing; and he kept the accounts.' In this each man echoes the parent that he takes after. They too were opposites, not merely in sex, but in class, upbringing, temperament, and nationality.

The twins live on a hill-farm which is bisected by the border between England and Wales. The two nations are complementary as well. The English landscape is softer and warmer than the Welsh uplands; the English characters are in general more cultivated (and devious) than the Welsh. But neither side is complete by itself; neither are the twins, if separated. This understanding is not arrived at sentimentally. In fact the two 'sides' – whether individuals or races – are shown to be more often than not at loggerheads. The English exploit the Welsh by crude appeals to patriotism and duty when volunteers are required in wartime – and the more aware of the Welsh know and resent it. On the domestic level Lewis Jones is angered by his twin brother's dependence on him. But, in the final analysis, the ties that bind together families, cultures, races – constricting as they may be – are shown as both inescapable and, in a curious manner, beneficial. The struggle in *On the Black Hill* is towards a wholeness that can never be achieved by an individual, or a people, in isolation. But it is a struggle: conflict is a necessary component of the search for completeness.

If *On the Black Hill* finally claims that union between opposites is the path to wholeness, then *Things Fall Apart* could be said to make the contrary case. This remarkable novel by Chinua Achebe describes tribal life in Nigeria in the last century, and the impact of whites, specifically missionaries, on that society. To summarize it in this way is to give the novel a misleading emphasis: the whites, some sensitive, some primitive in their interpretation of their task, appear only in the closing stages of the narrative and can be relegated to the status of minor figures. Nevertheless the effect they have on a static society is out of all proportion to their numbers.

Most of *Things Fall Apart* is given over to a celebration of that society. Superstitious, ritualized, very enclosed, it is profoundly alien to the Western reader. Achebe delivers his picture without explicit commentary. He does not sentimentalize his ancestors, and thereby make them superior to their conquerors; he does not show them as requiring at any level the technological intrusion of the whites; he shows them only as fundamentally distinct from the white interlopers. When they first encounter the missionaries the tribespeople are curious and ready to respond to their message. Many individuals see benefits, even if they're not those of religion:

There were many men and women in Umuofia who did not feel as strongly as Okonkwo about the new dispensation. The white man had indeed brought a lunatic religion, but he had also built a trading store and for the first time palm oil and kernel became things of great price, and much money flowed into Umuofia. (Chapter 21)

Many, naturally enough, are drawn by the greater comfort or profit that comes in the wake of the missionaries. It takes someone very resistant, obstinate or traditional, like Okonkwo, to stand against the trend. Okonkwo does not survive his involvement with the whites. Each reader must judge for him or herself exactly what weight to give to the closing chapters of *Things Fall Apart*. The story does not search for the reader's sympathy, but it is almost impossible to finish the novel without feeling that something of value has been lost in the death of this principal character.

Achebe demonstrates here that if two such opposed races and cultures meet then one of them will inevitably 'lose'; that is, will be assimilated by the culture that is more powerful, more persuasive, more cunning. While Chatwin in *On the Black Hill* sets out to suggest that harmony is ultimately attainable, Achebe shows that there can be no real understanding between cultures so radically different. The optimism of Chatwin's novel, although not easily won, can perhaps be accounted for by the fact that each 'side' at every level desires some kind of 'union' with its opposite; the boundary between them is no real fence, just a line on a paper map. For Achebe, however, there are no compromises; and the boundaries – of colour, of religious or cultural practice – are like brick walls. 'We' adopt 'their' values, 'they' adopt 'ours'. There is no middle path. This is a fact of history, or more precisely, a fact of life.

Conclusion

This examination of the results of conflict between cultures and races shows a range of possibilities. At the more hopeful end conflict can be seen as a precondition of harmony, the struggle of complementary opposites to adapt to each other before achieving, or coming near to, 'wholeness'. More usually any clash of this type will be judged in terms of winners and losers. In *The Merchant of Venice* or *Things Fall Apart*, very different works though they are, the conflict cannot be resolved by the artistic device of sensing a higher or transcendent union which will triumph over outward divisions. For Shakespeare, as for Achebe, one culture or system is going to predominate, and – deliberately or otherwise – will impose itself on the other. Somewhere in the middle of the spectrum falls a work such as *To Kill a Mockingbird*. Prejudice here is a very powerful force but it can be combated by enlightened and patient individuals (like Atticus Finch) who stand for what is best in their community. It is worth noting, however, that in Harper Lee's novel it is the ignorant or foolish white who has to adapt, that is, change his attitudes; the black man is presumed to have already done so, by virtue of his living in a largely white community and conforming to the majority's practices and expectations. There is therefore no real culture clash here; nor is the book intended to be a study of one. It is rather a condemnation of the misuse of power against a defenceless and honourable minority.

English coursework: Conflict

Assignments

1 Take a text discussed in this section, or any other appropriate work (such as *Cry, The Beloved Country* by Alan Paton), and explain whether it takes an optimistic or pessimistic view of racial or cultural conflict.

2 Discuss the different kinds of prejudice on display in Harper Lee's *To Kill a Mockingbird*.

3 From any of the texts discussed in this section take a character who is the victim of prejudice. In the first person – e.g. in a letter or a diary entry – write about a particular experience (either drawn from the text or invented) of prejudice.

4 You are the judge in the trial scene in *The Merchant of Venice*. What would have been your verdict on Shylock? Give reasons.

Revolution and rebellion

As one moves up the scale of conflict, the individual is lost from sight. Works that deal with whole societies in revolt or with countries at war are likely to be studies in history rather than what we usually recognize as 'literature'. As indicated earlier, the novelist or dramatist is best equipped to deal with individuals or small groups, even though these may be taken as representative of the larger forces at work.

Rebellion, revolution, war – all provide a highly dramatic context for a writer to work in. But the magnitude of the events may be overwhelming. At best a writer will only be able to *suggest* the scope of what is taking place rather than portray it in all its detail. As a parallel we should take the way a playwright copes with a battle on stage. He will either have to show a tiny bit of action and have it stand for the whole (Shakespeare does this frequently, in *Julius Caesar*, for example), or make the battle occur off-stage and have it recounted by a narrator (as occurs at the beginning of *Macbeth*), or resort to non-naturalistic devices such as lighting and sound effects to give an impression of a struggle. The one thing a dramatist can't do is reproduce, even in 'pretend' fashion, a battle in all its confusion, detail and scope. Of course we accept all this in a theatre without question, so much so that we may be surprised when Shakespeare apologizes through his Chorus in *Henry V* for presenting the battle of Agincourt with pitifully few players: 'four or five most vile and ragged foils,/Right ill-dispos'd in brawl ridiculous' (IV, Chorus, 50–1) – after all, what else could he do? Always in the theatre the audience is called upon to do a lot of the work with its imagination. In *Henry V* Shakespeare makes a virtue of necessity.

This is what most writers do when confronted by the large-scale conflict. They must concentrate on a small part of the canvas, but they may turn that limitation to an advantage. Since it is hard, if not impossible, to deal with people *en masse* in a novel or play (and even in the more 'realistic' medium of film), conflict on the national or international scale can only be realized at the level of the individual or the small group. And as individuals – whether as readers or members of an audience – this is what we best respond to. It is the individual predicament, the personal triumph, that touches the imagination or stirs the emotions, in literature, in a way that national dilemmas and victories never will.

A Tale of Two Cities (1859)

As an example of how a writer copes with events of historical significance I shall look at Charles Dickens' *A Tale of Two Cities*, the background to which is the French Revolution. Dickens makes a simple and powerful analysis of the causes of this nation-wide conflict. For centuries the ordinary people of France have been oppressed by a selfish aristocracy. At last they rise up against their tormentors and destroy them. But the fervour of the early days of the Revolution turns into a bloodthirsty terror, in which many innocent individuals are caught up and condemned. For Dickens the whole process has the inevitability of a natural law, and this is how he presents it: oppression – revolution – over-reaction. He deplores the later savage excesses of the revolutionaries but he cannot really be surprised at them; in frequent asides to the reader Dickens tells us that the people's cruelty has its origins in the monstrous cruelty and selfishness of the old ruling class.

This analysis is satisfactory to the reader. There is a moral and emotional reassurance in Dickens' dissection of the motives underlying the Revolution. But it's unlikely that such simple explanations would satisfy the historian, or the reader trying to establish factual truth. There is a mass of things that Dickens doesn't know or doesn't take into account about the Revolution. Given his purposes, this does not matter, for Dickens' focus is on a few individuals in the foreground of the picture. By choice, and by necessity, he can make up the background only with the broadest, simplest strokes of the brush. A sophisticated, detailed explanation of all the ascertainable causes of the French Revolution – social, economic, political – would be out of place.

If we look at a couple of episodes that provide part of the background, we see that Dickens is concerned not with subtlety and discriminating detail but with the general impression. In the following incident, set in Paris before the Revolution, a small child has been run over by the carriage of a marquis:

> The people closed round, and looked at Monsieur the Marquis. There was nothing revealed by the many eyes that looked at him but watchfulness and eagerness; there was no visible menacing or anger. Neither did the people say anything; after the first cry, they had been silent, and they remained so. The voice of the submissive man who had spoken, was flat and tame in its extreme submission. Monsieur the Marquis ran his eyes over them all, as if they had been mere rats come out of their holes.
>
> He took out his purse.
>
> 'It is extraordinary to me,' said he, 'that you people cannot take care of yourselves and your children. One or the other of you is for ever in the way. How do I know what injury you have done my horses? See! Give him that.'
>
> He threw out a gold coin for the valet to pick up, and all the heads craned forward that all the eyes might look down at it as it fell. The tall man called out again with a most unearthly cry, 'Dead!' ('Monseigneur in Town')

There is something of the caricature about this encounter. The Marquis, not given a name here, is a two-dimensional figure, an obvious villain who represents the corruption and selfishness of his class. There is no distinct perception of an individual. Dickens requires only that we understand something of the French people's loathing and fear of their 'superiors', and in this scene the nervy arrogance of the Marquis, the dumb but faintly threatening way the crowd encircle his carriage, together with impressions in others throughout the novel, swiftly sketch in the causes, and hint at the bloodiness of the conflict that will ensue.

Equally, when dealing with the other side to the conflict – the mass of the French people – Dickens treats them in general terms. During the storming of the Bastille, the crowd is seen as an elemental force, as powerful as the sea. But a crowd, or a mob, lacks individuality; it is one of the most frightening things about it. Dickens's very inability to focus on each person in the mob becomes in itself a telling feature of his descriptions. They are many, but they are also one, and it is the horrible unity of the mob, destroying and rejoicing, that points to some abandonment of essential human qualities. This is true of the Revolutionary dance, which is something closer to a frenzy:

Men and women danced together, women danced together, men danced together, as hazard had brought them together. At first, they were a mere storm of coarse red caps and coarse woollen rags ... They advanced, retreated, struck at one another's hands, clutched at one another's heads, spun round alone, caught one another and spun round in pairs, until many of them dropped ... Suddenly they stopped again, paused, struck out the time afresh, formed into lines the width of the public way, and, with their heads low down and their hands high up, swooped screaming off. No fight could have been half so terrible as this dance. ('The Wood-Sawyer')

In the excerpts Dickens conveys the quiet anger or demonic excitement of whole groups of people; elsewhere he paints scenes of the most violent conflict between classes. Yet, this, by itself, does not make a novel. Such scenes may be exciting, vivid, memorable, but they are largely without human interest. In fact, there is a deliberately *dehumanized* quality to the Revolutionary dance. These moments constitute the impressionistic background to *A Tale of Two Cities*, while the real drama of the narrative is provided by the predicaments of a dozen or so men and women trapped in the larger historical action. These aren't the anonymous 'men and women' described as dancing together frantically in the last quotation. The characters who involve us are individuals with names, lives, motives, fears and hopes. Through them the author can show, on a smaller, more properly human scale, his general insights into history: that cruelty and oppression will be paid for, that the reaction will be extreme and deaf to mercy, but that mercy and self-sacrifice are nevertheless potent attributes of human nature – ones to be discovered not in the distracted mob but in the private individual. In this respect it is significant that the climax to *A Tale of Two Cities* is an act of self-sacrifice, one man's dying in place of another. By this stage of the novel our sympathies have long since deserted the revolutionary cause, and we are on the side of the individual against the group.

It would be fair to claim that the bias of a novel or play is, in general, going to be in the direction already indicated – that is, towards the individual and away from the mass, the mob. In Dickens's account, the French people, tormented and heroic at the beginning, have become by the end a terrifying multi-headed monster shouting for blood and vengeance. Rebellion against, or resistance to, this 'monster' therefore becomes the praiseworthy course. We have already seen, in *The Crucible* and *A Man for All Seasons*, how the conflict between a man and his society can make for engrossing drama. In those plays, however, the conflict comes about largely as a result of inner turmoil: Thomas More and John Proctor are in debate with themselves before they enter, unwillingly, into battle with those around them. In other works, however, the emphasis is more firmly on the act of rebellion or resistance itself. These terms are distinct from what is implied by 'revolution'; rebellion and resistance can be private acts, revolution can't. In addition, the latter carries the idea of violent upheaval and change on a wide scale, while the former may return us to the individual and promises no certainty of change or success. In fact, a failed act of rebellion or resistance has an intrinsic drama or poignancy.

Brave New World (1932) and Nineteen Eighty-Four (1949)

This is well illustrated by two famous novels by Aldous Huxley and George Orwell respectively. In each story an individual stands out against oppressive or terrifying forces and his very act of resistance – passive though it may be – amounts to a kind of criticism of his society. A more unequal conflict couldn't be conceived: one against all the rest. Yet we feel at the conclusion of such struggles that a moral victory belongs to the individual, even as he pays the price of his individuality and is crushed by the weight of numbers against him. He is right, they are wrong.

In *Nineteen Eighty-Four* Orwell created a bleakly depressing picture of the future. The world is split into three enormous power blocs, perpetually at war with each other. England, renamed Airstrip One, is part of Oceania, a state where total conformity is demanded. Surveillance techniques are so sophisticated that the Thought Police can spy on the individual – in truth, there are few individuals left – by means of two-way telescreens installed in every room. Any 'incorrect' gesture or facial expression may be detected and punished. The state does not tolerate anyone who thinks for himself. To this end, all activity at variance with what is demanded by the ruling Party, and all real human responses (except fear and hatred) must be stamped out. To be, simply, an individual in such circumstances is to be a hero – and a criminal. Winston Smith is the central character of *Nineteen Eighty-Four*. His surname, the commonest in England, suggests his 'ordinariness', while 'Winston' recalls the dogged spirit of Churchill, Prime Minister during the Second World War; but he is no daring resistance fighter. Drawn on by a mixture of love, for Julia, a fellow-worker, and hatred, for the Party and what it represents, he becomes involved with what he believes to be an underground group fighting against the Party's tyranny. Winston is deluded and, in the end, alone. He is tortured into betraying his lover – or, more accurately, into betraying his love for her. *Nineteen Eighty-Four* is the book in which resistance fails, is shown to be futile, yet the very fact of its existence in one individual testifies to positive human values, however fragile.

What happens at the end of *Nineteen Eighty-Four* and *A Tale of Two Cities* is a defeat, although Dickens gives an air of Christ-like martyrdom to his protagonist. Such a defeat is, it would seem, the inevitable outcome of conflict between the individual and a violent or ruthless society. Yet the foregone nature of the conclusion does not detract from the drama or suspense of these narratives, and this fact suggests, once again, how natural we find it as readers or audience to identify with the plight of the individual.

Julius Caesar deals with resistance and rebellion, but, as has already been indicated by the discussion of Brutus's soliloquy, the foreground of the drama is taken up with a few men. Brutus is in conflict with himself, later in conflict with his fellow conspirator Cassius. The most exciting part of the play is not the assassination of Julius Caesar nor the battle at the climax of the civil war, but a battle of *words* between Brutus and Mark Antony. Each man addresses the Roman crowd (in Act III) after Caesar's death, the one explaining rationally and coolly why Caesar had to die, the other turning the crowd into a mob (Dickens would have recognized the process) by appeals to its greed and vengefulness. The point here is that action on a large scale – a mob storming the Bastille, two armies clashing on a plain – may actually be *less* dramatic than a contest of wills between two individuals, or the lonely resistance of a 'hero' withstanding brutal or remorseless pressures.

Assignments

1 Imagine yourself an English eye-witness at one of the scenes of mob violence described in *A Tale of Two Cities*. Write a letter home reflecting on what you have seen.

2 Make a comparison between George Orwell's *Nineteen Eighty-Four* and *Animal Farm*.

3 Read Aldous Huxley's *Brave New World*. How convincing do you find his vision of the future? Is it attractive in any way? Would you rebel against it?

4 Why do we identify with the individual against the group? Find examples from other books you have studied.

War: a chivalrous conflict

Of all forms of human conflict, the most absolute and destructive is warfare. Even a 'small' conventional war will end many lives, and the worst war we can imagine – a nuclear one – is literally the material of nightmares. Because art has to deal with all aspects of life, and especially with life in crisis, war is therefore an appropriate and inevitable preoccupation for writers – and is the basis of much prose, drama and poetry.

War has rarely been glorified in serious literature, and it would be most difficult to find a piece of twentieth century writing that approved of war *as such*, although there might be general agreement that a particular war had to be fought. If we return again to Shakespeare, however, we find in *Henry V* a drama that appears to endorse war as a means of expanding empire and as a convenient method of encouraging national pride and unity.

Henry V (1599)

Henry V is the final play in a cycle dealing with the reigns of three kings (with Richard II and Henry IV). Each work is different in terms of content, emphasis and style, but together they form a composite picture. In this panorama we see England enduring the turmoil of civil war and recovering its self-esteem and sense of purpose only when it turns its aggressive instincts outwards and exports them across the Channel. It is possible to be sceptical, even cynical, about the motives behind the war. Indeed, Shakespeare encourages such a response by introducing the Archbishop of Canterbury at the start of the play so that the churchman can give his holy authority to a war against France and provide a ludicrously complicated explanation of just why King Henry had a claim to the French throne. It is evident that the King is looking for a pretext to fight, and the campaign is a shrewd political move to unite a troubled nation rather than a moral crusade.

Nevertheless the war is presented in glowing, chivalrous terms – some of the time:

Now all the youth of England are on fire,
And silken dalliance in the wardrobe lies:
Now thrive the armourers, and honour's thought
Reigns solely in the breast of every man. (II Chorus, 1–4)

Henry's famous exhortations before the walls of the besieged town of Harfleur – 'Once more unto the breach, dear friends, once more ...' (III,1ff.) – and on the morning of Agincourt – 'We few, we happy few, we band of brothers' (IV,3,60ff.) – deal with courage, determination, the brotherhood of battle. As always in Shakespeare, more than one side of an issue is exposed. Not everybody in England is keen to go to war. There is a semi-comic sub-plot involving characters who are cowardly and parasitic on the body of the English army. There are traitors who plot to kill Henry before he departs for France. Prominent among the professional officer class are a Welshman, a Scotsman and an Irishman (so much for the *English* army!), like the figures in some joke concerning nationality.

But the most serious objection to the fighting is posed by an ordinary soldier whom the King encounters as he wanders in disguise through the camp to assess his men's morale. The argument is over the extent to which the obedience owed by a subject to his king frees that subject from any blame for fighting in a bad cause. The soldier says:

> But if the cause be not good, the king himself hath a heavy reckoning to make; when all those legs and arms and heads, chopped off in a battle, shall join together at the latter day, and cry all, 'We died at such a place'; some swearing, some crying for a surgeon, some upon their wives left poor behind them, some upon the debts they owe, some upon their children rawly left. I am afeard there are few die well that die in a battle; for how can they charitably dispose of any thing when blood is their argument? (IV,1,135–46)

What we remember from this speech is not so much the moral or philosophical point the soldier is making about the precise nature of the King's responsibility, but the strange picture he paints of severed limbs and heads reuniting at 'the latter day' (Judgement Day) and crying out as if still newly wounded on the battlefield. It is a forceful reminder that men die violently and agonizingly in warfare, and that they leave families mourning behind them – facts that cannot be completely glossed over in the talk of bravery and brotherhood. It is significant that the speech is delivered by a conscripted soldier, because he does not hope to earn the chivalrous esteem that might go to the knights at Agincourt, nor can he hope to profit by the war as some of the low-life comic figures expect to. In other words he has least to gain and most to lose.

In the final Act of *Henry V* the Duke of Burgundy is given a lengthy speech in which he elaborates on the destructive effect of war (V,2,23–67) – not merely destruction of the obvious sort, but more subtle ruin (fields are left uncultivated because the workers are fighting, the people as a whole grow uncultivated too because they lose the civilizing habit of peace). *Henry V* is not, however, an antiwar play, despite its occasional expression of scepticism. True, it shows that under the façade of national unity there will always be dissenters; it shows the fundamental destructiveness of war; but it also demonstrates that war brings out certain virtues in some of those who wage it. Above all, *Henry V* elevates its central character to heroic heights. After two weak or troubled kings, he is England's saviour, and the campaign against the French the means by which he restores his country's self-respect.

War: the modern view
Journey's End (1929) and *The Long and the Short and the Tall* (1959)

A play set during the First World War and another set in Malaya during the Second provide a very different view of war from that of *Henry V*. Shakespeare's work is expansive, all-inclusive: war may be Hell but it can also be a glamorous, chivalrous enterprise. In these plays by R. C. Sherriff and Willis Hall, war is dull misery or frightening action. There is bravery in both dramas but it is not celebrated in grand sweeping gestures against the enemy. These plays invite comparison; for example, each examines the manner in which men – there are no female characters – faced by the likelihood of death respond with a mixture of panic, humour, defiance and reminiscence.

Sherriff's play, *Journey's End*, covers a few days in an officers' dug-out. A German attack is imminent. There is no hatred of the enemy displayed. A newcomer to the front line asks, 'The Germans are really quite decent, aren't they? I mean, outside the newspapers?', and an experienced officer replies with a story about how a German officer not merely permitted them to carry a wounded man back to the British trench at night but actually fired 'some lights for them to see by'. Here is a kind of chivalry, readily acknowledged by the British officer, but the chivalry is seen not as some kind of attractive product, a flower of warfare, but as further proof of the absurdity of the whole business; in the public school language used in the dug-out it is all 'rather – *silly*'. *Journey's End* does not question the war itself (or, at least, such questions do not occur to Sherriff's characters), although there is some criticism of the selfishness and incompetence of the British higher command.

When we consider this First World War drama as an example of conflict a paradoxical situation arises. The enemy is not the real enemy. As already indicated, there is no overt hostility expressed towards the men in the front line opposite, who are after all just like them in being burdened with the same hateful task of killing or being killed. There is an implicit conflict in *Journey's End* between those who do the fighting and those who sit comfortably at a distance directing the battle. Yet this is much more strongly and bitterly expressed in other writing of this period. There is also explicit conflict between the various members of the same side – for instance, the senior officer, Captain Stanhope, finds himself at odds with the newcomer to his company and with another officer who pretends to be ill in an attempt to escape from danger. But even these scenes, dramatically effective though they are, do not dominate the action. This is a play about war in which, oddly enough, conflict does not seem to be the key issue. What is stressed rather are the ties of obligation and comradeship which bind together all the men – the captain, the coward, the company's 'joker'. In such a hellish environment just to maintain such notions of obligation and brotherhood becomes a quietly heroic act. Human beings have seemingly vanished from the wasteland they have created – Stanhope describes the front line as a dehumanized desert, without 'a sound or a soul; just an enormous plain ...'. To be human in a place like this is something that requires courage and endurance. Even then the strain of doing the 'decent' thing – a modest, blanket term which covers loyalty, bravery, being reliable, and so on – in such circumstances drives men to drink, neurosis, a welcoming attitude towards death.

The Long and the Short and the Tall, set less than thirty years later, inhabits a different 'social' world. Willis Hall's corporals and privates do not display the same enthusiasms or employ the public school phraseology of the World War I officers. Their predicament is much the same, though. Sheltering in a hut in the Malayan jungle they slowly realize that the Japanese, assumed to be many miles distant, are in reality about to overrun their position. The enemy here is perceived with a clarity and hostility not apparent in *Journey's End*. The Japanese are initially depicted, in the men's conversation, as fearful opponents. A lone enemy soldier stumbles across their hut and the problem of what to do with him takes up much of the second half of the action. The British soldiers view him in different ways but the prisoner (described in the stage direction as 'small, round, pathetic and almost comic') is the reverse of frightening. Confused, eager to curry favour with his captors, carrying photographs of his wife and children, he is uncomfortably like the men who have trapped him. By drawing this parallel Willis Hall heightens the soldiers' dilemma: do they kill this representative of the enemy in cold blood or do they take the risk of trying to get him back alive to their base in the midst of the advancing Japanese? One course is humanitarian but also far-sighted – because the prisoner may have valuable information; the other is ruthless, but also practical and perhaps even usual in such extreme circumstances of war. As in Sherriff's play, conflict here resolves itself into strife between men on the same side – one soldier defending the prisoner against the rest. In passing, we might note that a (German) prisoner of war puts in a brief appearance in *Journey's End* also – he too is terrified of his captors, and pathetically protective of a few personal belongings. The implicit point made by the dramatists in their treatment of the 'enemy' would appear to be that, however alarming or inhuman he is made out to be in newspapers or government propaganda, the individual soldier in reality is likely to be as baffled and frightened as the average member of the other side.

Contrasting these two works with Shakespeare's *Henry V* shows their prosaic, unglamorous view of war. War for Henry was the way to bind a kingdom's wounds and make it forget the self-inflicted injuries of civil war. The political union that is achieved between France and England at the conclusion is symbolized by the marriage of Henry to the French king's daughter. Here is a greater harmony brought about through conflict – even if the Chorus deflatingly indicates at the close that all the gains were lost in the reign of Henry VI. But the plays of this century have to search hard for war's justification. *Journey's End* doesn't even try. In *The Long and the Short and the Tall* the nearest any character gets to acknowledging that there is anything to fight for is when the sergeant admits that he hates making ruthless decisions (such as that the prisoner should be killed) but that someone has to do it; the alternative is to turn 'conshie' (be a conscientious objector) and 'leave the world to his lot' (the enemy forces). This is a very minimal, unpretentious motive for war; there is no glory to it.

Poetry of the First World War

It has already been suggested that the real venom of the fighting men, particularly in World War I, was reserved not for those in the line opposite but for those safely in the line to the rear. The poet and novelist Siegfried Sassoon, in a short, mocking poem about a commander who was well liked for his friendly manner, has two private soldiers express their approval of the General – 'He's a cheery old card'. Sassoon concludes the poem (titled 'The

General'): 'But he did for them both by his plan of attack.' This bitter little twist gives the lie to the officer's benevolent attitude, and suggests that he was, at best, incompetent; at worst, it makes him into a kind of murderer – as if he actually wanted the men under his command 'done for'. In the same way 'Base Details' (note the punning title) concludes a scathing attack on those who sit at a comfortable distance from danger, eating and drinking at base, while others die:

And when the war is done and youth stone dead.
I'd toddle safely home and die – in bed.

Once more the lines cast the harshest light on the higher command, insinuating that they really want to see all the young men dead and that only then will their job be complete. This is coupled with a contemptuous swipe at the cowardice and complacency of the major who 'toddles home' and whose death ('in bed' – notice the dash that delays the impact of the final phrase) is the acceptable consequence of old age.

The enemy here is plainly on the writer's own side. In other poetry of the period we understand that the enemy can be found in the elements or, indeed, the whole environment of war. Wilfred Owen is the most famous of the First World War poets; he was killed days before the Armistice that stopped the fighting in 1918. In 'Exposure' the weather is treated like an advancing army, and it is evident that boredom too, amounting to inertia, is another kind of enemy;

The poignant misery of dawn begins to grow ...
We only know war lasts, rain soaks, and clouds sag stormy.
Dawn massing in the east her melancholy army
Attacks once more in ranks on shivering ranks of grey,
   But nothing happens.

The abrupt falling away of the short final line suggests the feeling of anticlimax: almost anything would be better than this inactivity. The poem 'The Send-Off' describes the departure of a troop of men from their training camp in England. At the railway station

Dull porters watched them, and a casual tramp
Stood staring hard,
Sorry to miss them from the upland camp.
Then, unmoved, signals nodded, and a lamp
Winked to the guard.

The only human concern at their leaving comes from the unofficial figure of the tramp, and even this is mild – he is only 'sorry to miss them'. To the inanimate objects, the signal and the lamp held by a porter, Owen gives a disturbingly 'human' response. The signals 'nod', the lamp 'winks' as a hand or a shutter is lowered over it. The 'nod' and the 'wink' hint at a conspiracy, as if the items of equipment on the platform were really two people sharing a sinister or amusing secret which must be hidden from those around them. By extending a human movement or action, through the device known as personification, to objects which are incapable of feeling or of independent response, Owen suggests that everything in the soldiers' surroundings is involved in a kind of plot to get them sent away quickly and quietly. Why? Because these men are being sent to their deaths, and everybody – and everything – knows it. At one level the men themselves must be aware of it too. The reader might like to consider why the signals that 'nod' are also described in this verse as 'unmoved'.

One of Owen's most famous poems, 'Dulce et Decorum Est', is similarly a criticism of the hypocrisy and deceitfulness of those who stay behind and watch or encourage others to travel to their deaths. The poem, which should be studied in detail for its use of language and its rhythm, recounts a gas attack on a band of exhausted troops making their way to safety behind the front line. All but one manage to get their gas masks on in time. For the one who is too slow nothing can be done. Owen and his men are compelled to witness his slow agony ('His hanging face, like a devil's sick of sin'). The poem closes with a passionate plea: if you (the reader back in England) could have seen the victim dying, then

My friend, you would not tell with such high zest
To children ardent for some desperate glory,
The old Lie: Dulce et decorum est
Pro patria mori.

The Latin quotation, the saying that might be found at the foot of a war memorial, means 'it is sweet and fitting to die for one's native country'. The first four words provide the savagely ironic title to the poem; there is nothing remotely 'sweet' or 'proper' about this death. It is significant, in this respect, that the urgency of Owen's anger is directed, not against the Germans who sent over the gas-shells, nor against the armaments manufacturers, nor some other agency indirectly responsible for the attack, but fully at those who persist in telling lies about the nature of warfare and the duty of patriotism. This is further indication of the fact that First World War writers located their enemy not 'out there' but within their own camp.

Owen is, in general, less pointed in his criticism than is Sassoon. Owen's subject is ultimately the sense of tragic waste, the universal and futile suffering, 'the pity of war'. The phrase comes from 'Strange Meeting', a work that deals mysteriously – almost mystically – with a meeting between the poet and his opposite who is both 'enemy' and 'friend'. The poem seems to rise above old or conventional definitions of conflict. Similarly in 'The Next War' Owen moves beyond the usual notion of the enemy's being an identifiable group (the Germans, the British generals, the complacent propagandists back at home) to a conception of a time when men recognize their true enemy, not in other men, but in death itself. The vision is of humankind properly united, of a conflict worth engaging in, of a time

> when each proud fighter brags
> He wars on Death – for lives; not men – for flags.

Siegfried Sassoon, whose poetry has already been mentioned, took the same anti-authoritarian line in his semiautobiographical novel *Memoirs of an Infantry Officer*. George Sherston, whose progress in life is based on Sassoon's own, is a brave and modest man – see, for example, his account of capturing a German trench single-handed, in the section entitled 'Battle'. Sherston's courage extends to taking on the military and political establishment. He issues a statement, a copy of which he sends to his commanding officer. It includes such declarations as: 'I believe that this War, upon which I entered as a war of defence and liberation, has now become a war of aggression and conquest.' Sherston (and Sassoon, for this was actually the statement he published in real life) believes that the aims of the war have never been clearly expressed by the politicians, and he makes accusations of 'political errors and insincerities'. For his courage or foolhardiness Sherston/Sassoon was sent for treatment for shell-shock (i.e. mental breakdown), the army seeing this as a way of dealing with a difficult individual without having to answer any of his charges. Sassoon, like Owen, could be passionately angry, but his conflict was essentially with certain blind individuals in his own nation.

An examination of a poem by Edward Thomas, also killed in action in World War One, is included here for two reasons: it is well worth studying in its own right, and it demonstrates that writing about warfare does not have to deal directly with the battlefield or even to contain the bitterness or sense of tragedy that Owen and Sassoon give voice to. Thomas's fine poem 'As the Team's Head Brass' is given in full.

> As the team's head brass flashed out on the turn
> The lovers disappeared into the wood.
> I sat among the boughs of the fallen elm
> That strewed the angle of the fallow, and
> 5 Watched the plough narrowing a yellow square
> Of charlock. Every time the horses turned
> Instead of treading me down, the ploughman leaned
> Upon the handles to say or ask a word,
> About the weather, next about the war.
> 10 Scraping the share he faced towards the wood,
> And screwed along the furrow till the brass flashed
> Once more.
>   The blizzard felled the elm whose crest
> I sat in, by a woodpecker's round hole,
> 15 The ploughman said. 'When will they take it away?'
> 'When the war's over.' So the talk began –
> One minute more and the same interval.
> 'Have you been out?' 'No.' 'And don't want to, perhaps?'
> 'If I could only come back again, I should.
> 20 I could spare an arm. I shouldn't want to lose
> A leg. If I should lose my head, why, so,
> I should want nothing more... Have many gone
> From here?' 'Yes.' 'Many lost?' 'Yes, a good few.
> Only two teams work on the farm this year.
> 25 One of my mates is dead. The second day
> In France they killed him. It was back in March,
> The very night of the blizzard, too. Now if
> He had stayed here we should have moved the tree.'
> 'And I should not have sat here. Everything
> 30 Would have been different. For it would have been
> Another world.' 'Ay, and a better, though
> If we could see all all might seem good.' Then
> The lovers came out of the wood again:
> The horses started and for the last time

35 I watched the clods crumble and topple over
    After the ploughshare and the stumbling team.

   Thomas wrote widely of the English landscape, and it is likely this work sprang directly from a real encounter. In fact the poem looks at first like a direct transcription of the meeting with the ploughman; there is nothing very obviously 'poetic' in the account. Thomas catches faithfully the tone of everyday conversation in the short exchanges between himself and the farm-worker as he pauses before manoeuvring his plough down the next furrow. There's no violence or anger here. The scene is peaceful, orderly, gentle. And yet the war isn't really far off.

   Everything is subtly related to the destruction across the English Channel. Thomas sits on a fallen elm tree; the tree stays lying across the corner of the field because there are too few workers on the farm to clear it away; there are few workers because the men have enlisted (or been conscripted) to fight. The topic of the war inevitably comes up. 'Have you been out?' says the ploughman. He doesn't have to explain that he means out to France. Thomas's reply shows that he has considered the chances of getting wounded, he has even made up a list of what he might or might not spare ('I shouldn't want to lose/A leg.'). This type of speculation – fatalistic, macabre, a bit humorous as it's expressed here – must have been practised by all the men who were likely to be summoned to the front.

   The poem offers more, and it does so by a gentle suggestiveness. The tree fell in March during a blizzard. It was the very night the ploughman's mate was killed in France, the mate who would have helped to move the tree had he still worked on the farm. A link is established between the 'felling' of the man and of the tree, between the war and the blizzard. The war can be envisaged as an elemental force blowing down anything in its path; the tree is as helpless in the face of the weather's onslaught as the man is powerless in the face of battle. The interconnectedness of everything is hinted at also. One of the tiny consequences of the war is that the tree has not been shifted; one of the more important consequences (if minor in general terms) is that the ploughman has lost a fellow worker. Thomas is showing how conflict has remote, unforeseeable effects. The effects of war can be catastrophic, like the destruction of a blizzard, but they can also be almost imperceptible; Thomas would not be sitting on the fallen elm were it not for the war; the poem itself would not have the form it does were it not for the war.

Despite the destructive impact of the conflict the ploughman does not hate it. Thomas points out that if the war had not occurred the world would have been different, 'another world'. The initial response is to say that it would – of course – have been a 'better' world, but the ploughman concludes optimistically that 'if we could see all all might seem good'. The line hints tentatively that even an event as destructive, as subtly ruinous as war may have its place in the scheme of things, and that we are not really equipped to judge or to condemn, because we cannot see all (not having a God's-eye view of the world?). The reader must assess for him or herself whether such optimism is too straightforward – one wonders what Owen or Sassoon's response would have been to the ploughman's words. The context of the meeting between poet and ploughman is a consoling one – the act of ploughing itself, and the disappearance of the lovers into the wood from which they emerge at the end give a kind of 'frame' to the dialogue. They also indicate that even in the middle of a war certain indispensable human activities, of life rather than death, will continue.

Assignments

1 Compare and contrast *Journey's End* and *The Long and the Short and the Tall*.

Suggested notes for your answer: Both plays focus on all-male groups of characters over few hours/days – show how men respond to near certainty of death – conflict springs from differences of temperament within groups, and friction between those in command and those under them – conflict not much to do with 'official' enemy; very different language used in each play (uniform 'public school' tone in *Journey's End*, variety of accents in *LST*) – does this make for greater realism in WWII drama? – does either play provide any justification for war?

2 Why does Henry go to war with France in *Henry V*? Is he right to do so?

3 Write a letter home from an ordinary English soldier on the night before the battle of Agincourt.

4 Read the poems by Owen and Sassoon referred to in the last few pages. Which, in your view, most effectively conveys the writer's hatred of war, and why?

5 Give a critical account of any text involving war other than those discussed in this section (for example, *All Quiet on the Western Front* (E. M. Remarque), *Catch-22* (J. Heller)). What seems to be the author's attitude towards his subject matter?

War: nuclear conflict

The conflict of 1914–18 was thought to be the war to end wars, so immense was the scale of death and ruin. Yet the toll of World War II was greater still, and 1945 saw the beginning of the atomic age when bombs were dropped on the Japanese cities of Hiroshima and Nagasaki. Since that moment fear of an ultimate conflict has haunted humanity, and literature – like other art forms – has made uncertain attempts to deal with it.

John Hersey's *Hiroshima* (1946), written originally for an American magazine, is a collection of six portraits of individual Japanese – doctor, priest, soldier's widow, etc – who happened to be in Hiroshima on the morning of 6 August 1945. These eye-witness accounts of the experience of what was, by present standards a small nuclear explosion, come without explicit commentary from the author. He 'merely' lets the people and the events speak for themselves. But the act of focusing on a group of men and women who are 'average' citizens is a reminder that, even if the scale of destruction is such that we register only the noughts at the end of the casualty figures, every unit in that total stands for an individual whose life has been stopped or, at the least, violently transformed by catastrophe.

Perhaps the least unsatisfactory way to deal with nuclear conflict is in this documentary fashion, although a number of novelists have tackled a topic that tends to induce – in writer and reader alike – a feeling of horror or helplessness. Nevil Shute's *On the Beach* (1957) foresees a cloud of radioactivity from war fought in the northern hemisphere slowly creeping down to the southern regions of the globe. The people of Australia, the setting of the novel, know that they are condemned and can do nothing but while away the time as extinction approaches. A less pessimistic narrative is *The Chrysalids* (1955) by John Wyndham. This is a work of science fiction, located in a world many thousands of years in the future after a catastrophe termed Tribulation (i.e. nuclear war) has struck. Humanity survives in small primitive communities but the need to guard against the genetic mutations caused by fallout has led to a very superstitious and oppressive society from which anything 'abnormal' is banished. The novel dramatizes the predicament of a group of young people who come to question their society's values, and recounts their eventual escape. Like Wyndham's other books *The Chrysalids* is an examination of how people respond and adapt to extraordinary conditions. It also offers a study of conflict on several levels.

Summing up

It should be apparent from what you have read so far that conflict, as a topic in literature, is complex and inescapable. Whenever an individual is divided against himself, or is in dispute with others, or where groups of people are set against opposing groups, there is conflict. And conflict is at the core of drama, whether we are using that term in the restricted sense of 'theatre' or applying it more broadly to describe all writing (and film, etc) which is characterized by strong feeling and a sense of intensified reality. To call something 'dramatic' makes it matter. This is why newspapers employ headlines such as 'Hostage Drama' or television shows footage of a '*dramatic* rescue bid'. In such events we understand that the routine of daily life is suspended, and that something unusual is occurring in which people are at risk. These are obvious examples of the 'dramatic'. But whether one is describing these or instances of quieter drama (as, for example, an individual's inner struggle with himself over some necessary choice), the heart of the drama is conflict. As indicated at the beginning of this study, for a contest of any kind to earn the title of conflict there must be some agreement that the outcome of that contest is of significance. If neither side in an argument actually cares about winning – or isn't afraid of losing – then the argument is not an important one. At the least, it cannot be presented with full dramatic impact.

This is not to say that the reader has to judge a conflict by the same standards as the participants in it. In fact we may be encouraged to do the very reverse: to see how wasteful or absurd a dispute or battle is. The case of Pope's *Rape of the Lock* has already been mentioned in the Introduction. Here we are meant to realize that there are no proper grounds for conflict; that it exists tells us something about the pride or pettiness of human nature. A parallel case is provided by a book of the same period as Pope's poem, *Gulliver's Travels* by Jonathan Swift. This contains a satirical (that is, comic, ironic) description of a war between two imaginary kingdoms, Lilliput and Blefuscu. This is how this very silly dispute began:

Summing up

It is allowed on all Hands, that the primitive way of breaking Eggs before we eat them, was upon the longer End: But his present Majesty's Grand-father, while he was a Boy, going to eat an Egg, and breaking it according to the ancient Practice, happened to cut one of his Fingers. Whereupon the Emperor his Father published an Edict, commanding all his Subjects, upon great Penalties, to break the smaller End of their Eggs. The people so highly resented this Law, that our Histories tell us, there have been six Rebellions raised on that Account ... These civil Commotions were constantly fomented by the Monarchs of Blefuscu ... It is computed, that eleven Thousand Persons have, at several Times, suffered Death, rather than submit to break their Eggs at the smaller End. (Part One, Chapter 4)

The immediate application of this satire is to the conflict between Catholics and Protestants and the countries which were their respective strongholds, France (Blefuscu) and England (Lilliput). Plainly there is a desperate absurdity in people fighting and dying over which end an egg should be broken. There might seem to be an absurdity too over members of the same religion going to war with each other. But, more generally, Swift is emphasizing and deploring the human tendency to find occasion for conflict in the smallest, most trivial differences. Both Swift and Pope alert us to our natures; both encourage us to laugh at it (the alternative might be tears).

An examination of Swift should encourage the reader to think about some of the different approaches that can be brought to bear on conflict. In *Gulliver's Travels* (religious) war is perceived as something ridiculous – because of the insignificance of its causes. Yet to writers of the First World War period, the conflict and its origins (which may be futile or ridiculous) are not material for laughter. Why is this? Look carefully at the differences in tone between the chapter in *Gulliver's Travels* from which the passage is taken and a passage describing a casualty in battle from, say, Sassoon's *Memoirs of an Infantry Officer*. What are the different purposes of each writer? Are they, in their various ways, equally serious?

Don't assume that when a writer deals with conflict he will condemn it, as a matter of course. This is true, even of the most tragically wasteful forms. Remember the ploughman's words in Edward Thomas's 'As the Team's Head Brass' – if only because they encourage us to take a view that is a little different, not the reflex reaction. Many of the examples touched on in this study, in fact, indicate the positive or creative aspects of conflict. Pip in *Great Expectations* achieves a resolution to his problems that will satisfy himself (and the reader) only after undergoing a series of conflicts with himself and with others. There is no other way in which his self-realization will be attained, no other path to growth except 'battle'. Conflict here may be painful, but it is healthy and vital. Similarly the family struggles dramatized in a variety of texts – from D. H. Lawrence's *Sons and Lovers* to Stan Barstow's *A Kind of Loving* – are both inevitable and, in some ways, productive. Growth and change are essential to narrative momentum, and they will not come about except through conflict.

When considering a story or a play or a poem in the light of this theme the student must first decide exactly what sort of conflict he or she is dealing with, and then assess its value. Do we agree with the goals of an individual in conflict? Do we feel that he is deceiving himself (like Brutus in *Julius Caesar*)? How far does the author appear to agree with, or distance himself from his protagonist (as Mark Twain does when Huckleberry Finn argues with himself over betraying the runaway slave)? How does language assist us in determining what to think and feel? Expect subtlety, expect to have to *think*!

There are further dimensions – many of them – not touched on in this study. As an example, one might take conflict between appearance and reality, the clash between the way things look and the way they really are (the basis of irony). Theatre by its very nature encourages questions of this sort. Plays such *The Servant of Two Masters* (by Carlo Goldoni) or *Billy Liar* (by Willis Hall and Keith Waterhouse) deal with fantasy, confusion of identity, uncertainty: all are fuel for a consideration of conflict. And an aspect of conflict that hasn't been much to the fore in this book – its *comic* potential. Above all, appreciate for yourself the breadth, variety and excitement of this fundamental literary theme.

General questions

1 In what ways can conflict be said to be 'healthy'? Give examples from what you have read.

Suggested notes for essay answer:
Conflict not necessarily destructive, at least at individual level. It may be stimulating, life-enhancing to participate in or witness (some) situations of conflict – we're compelled to defend our ideas, beliefs, feelings, and may (should?) be changed by the experience. A book that challenges us is more exciting than one that fits in with our prejudices. Greater clarity or understanding may come about when conflict has been resolved, either inner (Pip in *Great Expectations*) or outer (warring husband and wife in *A Kind of Loving*). Even if the 'wrong' side wins, as with Macbeth, the fight can still be worthwhile – the fact that Macbeth does struggle with himself gives evidence of 'good' aspect of his nature (and so increases tragedy of what follows, because he could have turned in a different direction). Here conflict underlines sense of human freedom or potential. Further up the scale, it's difficult to find 'healthy' or redeeming features – in war, for example, where scale of destruction is likely to outweigh small gains.

2 Take a trial scene from one of the texts referred to in this study (*To Kill a Mockingbird, The Crucible, A Man for All Seasons, The Merchant of Venice*) or from any other appropriate text you have read, and using it as a base explain why a conflict in court makes for good reading/watching.

3 Find examples of the use of the terms 'good' and 'evil' in the media (look especially in the tabloid papers). Explain why they have been used, and what is conveyed to you by them.

4 Taking one of the texts about war as a starting point (for instance, Siegfried Sassoon's poems), write a dialogue between an officer and a private soldier.

5 Compare a situation of family conflict in which you have been involved with a similar situation in a book you have read. Looking back, do you feel differently to the way you did at the time?

6 Write about what it feels like, or would feel like, to be a member

English coursework: Conflict

of a minority group, using one of the texts discussed in this study as a base.

7 Choose one of the books dealing with nuclear war mentioned in the last section (or find another of your own choice). Do you consider that the author has found any positive features in what he depicts? What points does the book make for you?

8 Take a scene from any of the plays discussed in this study and describe carefully how you would stage it so as to bring out the underlying conflict.

9 Watch a filmed (or televised) version of any of the books mentioned here, and compare it with the original. What has been gained or lost?

10 Find an example of a text providing humorous conflict. What makes it funny?

Some suggested further reading

The titles given below, many of them on GCSE and A-level exam syllabuses, will provide material when you are dealing with the topic of conflict. They are arranged by author, alphabetically, and not according to the categories of conflict referred to in this study. After some an indication of the kind of conflict involved has been given.

Prose

Jane Austen *Pride and Prejudice*
Emily Brontë *Wuthering Heights* (family/sexual)
Anthony Burgess *A Clockwork Orange* (good/evil)
Joyce Cary *Mister Johnson* (racial/cultural)
Dan Davin (editor) *Night Attack* (short stories from the Second World War)
Len Deighton *Bomber*
  Declarations of War
Charles Dickens *David Copperfield*
  Hard Times (industrial)
E. M. Forster *A Passage to India* (racial/cultural)
Robert Graves *Goodbye to All That* (war)
Graham Greene *Brighton Rock* (good/evil)
  The Power and the Glory
  The Third Man (conflict of loyalties)
Thomas Hardy *Far from the Madding Crowd* (love)
  The Mayor of Casterbridge
Joseph Heller *Catch-22* (war)
Ernest Hemingway *A Farewell to Arms* (love/war)
  The Old Man and the Sea
Barry Hines *A Kestrel for a Knave*
C. S. Lewis *That Hideous Strength* (good/evil)
  Voyage to Venus (good/evil)
George Orwell *Animal Farm* (revolution)
  Coming Up for Air
  Homage to Catalonia (war)
Erich Maria Remarque *All Quiet on the Western Front*
Alan Sillitoe *Saturday Night and Sunday Morning* (personal/class)
John Steinbeck *Of Mice and Men*
  The Grapes of Wrath (class)

English coursework: Conflict

Evelyn Waugh *Decline and Fall* (comic)
  A Handful of Dust (sexual/comic)
John Wyndham *The Day of the Triffids*

Drama

Oliver Goldsmith *She Stoops to Conquer* (deception/comic)
Bill Naughton *Spring and Port Wine* (family)
John Osborne *Look Back in Anger* (family/class)
  Luther (religion/family)
Shakespeare *Romeo and Juliet* (love/family)
George Bernard Shaw *Saint Joan* (religion/war)
  The Devil's Disciple (rebellion)
Peter Terson *Zigger Zagger* (class/cultural)
Oscar Wilde *The Importance of Being Earnest* (comic)

Poetry

It is difficult to recommend individual poems. You might, however, look in anthologies for other appropriate material by writers already discussed in this study, namely, Seamus Heaney, Wilfred Owen, Siegfried Sassoon, Edward Thomas. Also search for poetry by Ted Hughes, Philip Larkin, D. H. Lawrence.

Relevant Brodie's Notes

A Kind of Loving
A Man for All Seasons
Jane Eyre
On the Black Hill
Great Expectations
Lord of the Flies
The Long and the Short and the Tall
Sons and Lovers
To Kill a Mockingbird
The Crucible
Nineteen Eighty-Four
An Inspector Calls
Julius Caesar
Macbeth
The Merchant of Venice